Cider with Laurie
Laurie Lee Remembered

Barbara Hooper

Cider with Laurie
Laurie Lee Remembered

PETER OWEN PUBLISHERS
London & Chester Springs

◢

B LEE
1446138

PETER OWEN PUBLISHERS
73 Kenway Road, London SW5 0RE

Peter Owen books are distributed in the USA by Dufour Editions Inc.,
Chester Springs, PA 19425-0007

First published in Great Britain 1999
© Barbara Hooper 1999

ISBN 0 7206 1075 3

A catalogue record for this book is available from the British Library

Printed in Great Britain by Hillman Printers (Frome) Ltd

The poem 'All for Laurie Lee' is reprinted by permission of
The Peters Fraser and Dunlop Group Ltd on behalf of Roger McGough;
© as printed in the original volume

For
Kenneth, Stephen, Martin,
Julian and Benjamin

Acknowledgements

I would like to thank the executors of Laurie Lee's estate and his literary agents for giving me permission to proceed with this book, begun before he died, and Kathy Lee, his widow, for answering my questions. My thanks go also to relatives of Laurie Lee who gave me insights into various aspects of his life: Howard Beard, Yasmin David, Jack Lee, Charles Light, Frances Light, Marion Light and Diana Roper.

For the London years I had help from Christopher Barry, Gill Chambers, Sean Day-Lewis (who also generously allowed me to quote from his biography of his father), Christopher Fry, Richard Last, Lady Monson (Emma Devas), John Mortimer, Katie Paltenghi, Alan Ross, Bernard Stone, Jan Treacy, Lady Tucker (Jacqueline Thomson) and Stephanie Walmsley. Others who responded to my inquiries included Charles Causley, Peter Levi and Roger McGough.

In Gloucestershire I am grateful to the following people: Vera Chapman, Johnny Coppin, U.A. Fanthorpe, Jim Fern, Royston and Marjorie Fry, Shelagh Hancox, Michael Holloway, Adam Horovitz, P.J. Kavanagh, Elizabeth Kirby, Patrick Love, Kirsty Mugford, Alan Payne, Sonia Rolt, Jack Russell, Jack Sollars, Barbara Tait, Barbara Tittensor, Alan and Joan Tucker and Arthur Swain. Not surprisingly, visits to the Woolpack Inn always yielded new inspiration.

During my visit to Spain I had invaluable help from José Andreas, Juan Manuel de Haro, David and Anna Kenning, Manuel Mateos, Diana Matheson and Máximo Lorriel Ruiz. Julian Brown was my interpreter, and for information relevant to Laurie Lee's experiences in the Civil War I am indebted to Jack Jones and Barry McLoughlin.

I am grateful to my editor, Antonia Owen, and to Gill Mittins, Anne Puckridge and Jim Ruston for help in assembling the manuscript and photographs.

Relevant archive material was made available at the Public Record Office (Kew), the Dorset County Record Office (Dorchester), the Gloucester County Record Office (Gloucester), the Imperial War Museum (Lambeth) and the Family Records Centre (Islington). The staff of Stroud Public Library were most efficient at locating out-of-print books, and I also received assistance from the Jack Russell Gallery at Chipping Sodbury.

My thanks go to all of them.

Nunca vi gentes tan alegres.
Cantaban levantando el vino
por la salud y por la muerte . . .
Regresé a mi casa más viejo
después de recorrer el mundo.

– Pablo Neruda,

'¿Y cuánto vive?' from *Estravagario* (1958)

Preface

We are sitting in the back bar of a small English country pub. I am with an old man, smartly dressed, half blind, hard of hearing. His manner is courteous and a little quirky. On the table is an untouched half-pint of beer. He speaks with a trace of a Gloucestershire burr, only recognizable if you are used to hearing the local speech. In a plastic shopping bag he has a book, already signed with a personal message, which he gives me as we say goodbye.

We discuss his life, his travels, his view of the world he has watched changing around him; but, above all, his village, the village in which he was born and has spent fifty-four of his eighty-one years. He orders cider for me from the landlord. Good-humoured and entertaining, he becomes more passionate when the conversation turns to traffic congestion, ugly new building developments, privatized companies or other aspects of the modern world he dislikes.

He talks with the idiom and vision of a poet and the wisdom of having lived through most of the great events of the twentieth century and having written about many of them. This is Laurie Lee, settled in his accustomed place in the Woolpack Inn at Slad, in the Gloucestershire Cotswolds. We are a stone's throw from his childhood home. I had known and loved his poems for many years, and the book he now gives me is an illustrated edition of *Cider with Rosie*, the story of his early years, the story that made him a legend.

Two years later, a funeral is taking place in Holy Trinity Church at

Slad. It is an unostentatious village ceremony, with a traditional service led by the vicar. Yet the exceptional number of mourners and the mass of flowers would suggest to passers-by that someone rather special has died. One pyramid of lilies carries a silver card: 'To our Dear Friend from your friends in Spain, Juan Carlos and Rosa, Michael and Helga, and all the village of Almuñécar.' Afterwards the mourners gather at the Woolpack, where folk music is played and beer and cider flow lavishly. The people of Slad have buried Laurie Lee in their local churchyard, midway between the church and the inn, exactly as he wished.

Five months on and a distinguished congregation gathers at St James's Church, Piccadilly, in London's West End, to participate in a memorial service for the writer. There are tributes from the Labour MP David Blunkett, a diplomat (the Irish ambassador to Spain), the musician Bobby Kok, poets and playwrights including John Mortimer, P.J. Kavanagh and Brian Patten. A Canon of Gloucester Cathedral reads Laurie's best-known poem, and the London Chamber Orchestra plays his favourite piece of music by Haydn. Two eminent poets, Christopher Fry and Roger McGough, read verses they have written in memory of Laurie. Most movingly, the congregation listens to a scratchy, indistinct recording of Laurie playing a Spanish tune on his violin.

Three very different events illustrating some of the facets of this many-coated man, famous around the world, who now lies at rest in his Cotswold valley.

Contents

List of Illustrations
between pages 102 and 103

Laurie at his stepsister Dorothy's wedding, 1927

Laurie in Morocco, 1948

Views of Slad as it is today: the village seen across the valley; Mrs Lee's Cottage, now called Rosebank; Holy Trinity Church; Steanbridge Lake; the former schoolteacher's house; the old village school

The Woolpack Inn

Laurie at a party celebrating the opening of the PEN Club's new headquarters, 1949

Laurie in his role as Curator of 'Eccentrics' Corner' and Caption-Writer-in-Chief at the Festival of Britain, photographed in 1950

Laurie receives prize money from Dame Peggy Ashcroft for the W.H. Smith and Son Annual Literary Award, 1960

Laurie and Kathy, 1960

Laurie judging a beauty contest, 1963

Laurie relaxing with Kathy and Jessy, 1964

Laurie and other regulars at the Queen's Elm, 1976

Laurie promoting his books in Stroud, 1992

The author of Cider with Rosie was born on the eve of the First World War and lived until three years before the end of the twentieth century. The south Gloucestershire valleys in which he was born and grew up imprinted themselves on his mind's eye for the whole of his life. In middle age he was able to re-create his early childhood in a way that speaks to everyone who remembers growing up in a country village and makes envious many who did not.

He was an eye-witness to the Spanish Civil War. He lived through the London Blitz during the Second World War. He produced poetry, prose, plays and government reports and wrote for radio and television. All three volumes of his autobiography became best-sellers. And everything he wrote was underpinned by his poems, by the rural images and sensory impressions he carried with him as part of his heritage.

His evocation of his two years in Spain are coloured by Cotswold contrasts. His historical drama set in the Middle Ages also draws on memories of this part of the English countryside, its seasons and its teeming life. Almost every poem he wrote owes its inspiration to that landscape.

For many, Laurie Lee is synonymous with Gloucestershire, yet what he wrote has a universality and speaks of the human condition on a much wider canvas. Readers of his work see the world as he saw it, rooted in an English valley.

1

The Lees and the Lights

Walking the abandoned shade
of childhood's habitations,
my ears remembering chime,
hearing their buried voices.
       – 'The Abandoned Shade'

AN unremarkable Cotswold stone house, T-shaped and rather dilapidated, lies tucked below a grass bank by the main road in a pleasant but unremarkable village. This is one of the most familiar family homes in modern English literature. It stands at the heart of *Cider with Rosie* and in the centre of the small Gloucestershire village of Slad, in a steep valley on the edge of the limestone Cotswold hills where they begin to climb up from the Severn Vale and the Bristol Channel. This is the landscape of Laurie Lee, just as Dorset is Hardy country or the north Yorkshire moors are associated with the Brontës.

Laurie Lee wrote in *Cider with Rosie* that he remembered his life from when he was lifted down from a carrier's cart in the middle of Slad at the age of three. But his family roots reach back much further into south Gloucestershire, into the landscape which defined so many of his poems as well as his autobiography.

His maternal grandfather, John Light, was a coachman at the small market town of Berkeley in the Vale, mainly ferrying passengers from the Berkeley Arms to Gloucester or the new railway station at Berkeley Road Junction. Berkeley was where Edward II was murdered and the birthplace of Edward Jenner who pioneered vaccination; it is also the setting for one of Gloucestershire's four medieval castles. The castle dominated a stretch of the water meadows alongside the river Severn, where it opens out into the Bristol Channel, much as the Sharpness nuclear power station dominates the river flats today.

By the time John started work Berkeley Castle had watched over the valley for eight hundred years. Henry II had granted a charter there to Robert Fitzhardinge, a third-generation Norman knight. In John Light's time the lord of Berkeley was Charles, Baron Fitzhardinge, who lived from just before Queen Victoria came to the throne until the First World War.[1]

In 1892 the local directory drew attention to Berkeley's prestige. It was 'a town, seaport and parish' with gas lighting, a cottage hospital, two reading rooms and a library.[2] A horse-drawn omnibus met every train at Berkeley Road Station, and John seems to have progressed to this more up-to-date form of transport as coach driver.

This was the late Victorian community in which Laurie's mother grew up. It is likely that John occasionally drove guests up to the castle, and he may have had even closer links there. Laurie wrote that his mother, Annie Light, impractical, incurably romantic, excitable and book-loving, 'had some mysterious connection with the Castle, something vague and intimate, half-forgotten – who knows what? – implying a blood-link somewhere'.

In 1858 John married Emma Morse of Gloucester, and Annie Light was born at Quedgeley in the spring of 1879, the only girl in a family of six. Quedgeley, a village on the outskirts of Gloucester, about three miles from Berkeley, had a population of roughly four hundred when Annie was a child. Local men worked on the Gloucester and Berkeley Ship Canal, and Annie as a girl may have heard some seamen's tales which she passed on to her children. There was a National School for 120 children which she attended, where her intelligence caught the eye of the schoolmaster, who gave her extra tuition so that she grew up better educated than most of her village friends.

A photograph taken near Quedgeley Church in about 1890 shows Annie as a tall, long-haired girl with three of her brothers, one in a wheelbarrow – a happy and well-dressed family group.

At thirteen, however, it was necessary for her to leave school to help look after the family. Her mother was ill and the family was hard up. Then, like so many of her generation in rural England, she went into domestic service. It was common practice for girls as young as fourteen to take up residential jobs in large country houses. The advantage of free board and lodging enabled them to send home their wage packet, typically £5 a year – a fair boost to a struggling family's income. Annie's childhood was over.

Laurie wrote of his mother working as a scullery-maid, nurse-maid and parlour-maid in West Country manor houses. Years later she would relive the more memorable incidents during her upstairs-downstairs years among 'the gentry' in the tales she told her children. She dreamed her dreams, and if they included imagining herself the secret offspring of a nobleman, or having an Indian prince fall in love with her, there was not much harm in that.

Annie fanned the flames of imagination for Laurie, with her fireside stories and her passions: filling in scrapbooks, collecting job lots of battered porcelain at country house auctions, working on her jungle-like garden, playing the piano, entering newspaper competitions and cycling erratically up and down the valley.

Laurie paid tribute to his mother in *Cider with Rosie:* 'I absorbed from birth, as now I know, the whole earth through her jaunty spirit.' On his mother's side he also inherited a spirit of adventure and a love of travel, for the Lights were an enterprising family.

By 1906 John had given up his coaching job and his work with horses. As trains and motor buses took over, horse transport became redundant. He found a job as a beer retailer in the tiny south Cotswold village of Sheepscombe, across the valley from more prosperous Painswick and some five miles from the mill town of Stroud. After her mother's death Annie left the last of her stately homes, with mixed feelings, to keep house for her widowed father.

Apart from Annie, John had five sons, collectively called 'the uncles' by Laurie, each of whom fought in the trenches during the First World War. All five survived, against the odds, and prospered in different occupations at home and abroad.

Sheepscombe at the turn of the century had a population of barely four hundred, yet it supported three inns: the Butchers' Arms, the Crown and John Light's beerhouse (not listed officially but known locally as the Plough). The Plough survives as a whitewashed three-storey building, with its name and the bracket for the inn sign, but now it is a private house on the road from Jack's Green to The Camp.

Before the war village beerhouses were, to rural workers, refuge, entertainment and often their only place of relaxation. Usually consisting of a room in a cottage, they were a more basic kind of hostelry than inns (where a night's lodging could be had), and drunkenness and fights were not uncommon – hardly surprising, given that a glass of beer or rough cider cost a penny and a tot of rum tuppence.

As well as being housekeeper to her father and brothers, Annie during her twenties was also barmaid at the Plough – two very demanding roles. She learned to throw trouble-makers out into the road and make up a straw bed in the stables for exhausted travellers. Eventually she felt the need for independence, and Laurie told how she answered an advertisement placed the local newspaper, the *Stroud News*, by a young widower requiring a housekeeper to look after his five motherless children: 'And that's how she met my father.' An advertisement did indeed appear in the Situations Vacant and Wanted column on 30 September 1910: 'Good general servant wanted in Stroud District. Small family. Apply by letter in first place to M.L., Stroud News Office.' Five children was a small family by Edwardian standards.

Annie applied, got the job and moved into Reg Lee's narrow red-brick villa, Glenview, on the Slad Road in Uplands. This was more or less a suburb of Stroud on the Gloucester side, no more than three miles from Slad. Glenview is still there, rather shabby, with its name clearly visible in stone at first-floor level. It is reached by some steps from the road with a small garden in front and behind. Evidently Annie proved a satisfactory housekeeper and child-minder for, in the traditional way, she married her employer. The wedding was held on 11 May 1911 at the newly built All Saints Church, Uplands.

The groom was described as a widower and grocer's manager, aged thirty-four, and he seems to have worked for the Co-op grocery just down the road. The bride was identified as Annie Emily Light, spinster, aged thirty-two. The register was signed by George Frederick Light – Annie's brother Fred – and by Edith C. Swain, a Painswick friend.

Was it purely a marriage of convenience for Reg? There were four children from this second marriage, but the parents stayed together for barely four years. Neither of them ever remarried. Annie adored Reg, and Laurie said that the separation broke her heart.

While Annie was evidently imaginative and creative and passed these qualities on to her son, it is harder to detect the characteristics Laurie inherited from his father's side. The Lees are rather shadowy figures in his writings, less well documented than the Lights. They moved to Gloucestershire from Dorset only in the 1890s. They were seafaring rather than farming folk, and this must have contributed to Laurie's wanderlust as a young man. Lees had lived in the Bridport area of Dorset from the seventeenth century, working in traditional seaport occupations such as sailing, rope-making and flax-weaving to make sailcloth.[3]

Reg Lee's grandfather, Elijah Lee, born in 1822, had sailed with a coastal vessel called the *Why Not?* The *Why Not?* traded out of Bridport when it was a busy harbour, plying mainly between Sunderland, Bridport and Guernsey with cargoes of coal. She was a two-masted schooner built in Sweden in 1849 but enlarged at Bridport five years later. Normally she carried a crew of twelve to fifteen, and Elijah was her captain during the 1860s. Records show that the *Why Not?* was wrecked off the north coast of Scotland in 1881 with the loss of all hands. Fortunately Elijah was no longer a crew member, and at about this time he moved to Cardiff with his second wife and some of his six children.

Reg's father, William Joseph Lee, was born at Bridport in 1848, the third of Elijah's sons. His occupation is recorded on his marriage certificate as seaman on the motor vessel *Hector*, but there is no later record of his being at sea, and apparently none of Elijah's family maintained the seafaring tradition. William married a local girl, Emma Hallett from Burton Bradstock, and they had two sons, George and Reginald. Reg, Laurie's father, was born at Askerswell, a village near Bridport, in 1877.

Between 1881 and 1891 three of Elijah's sons left Bridport for Stroud with their families. The oldest, Frederick, had been apprenticed as a tailor and moved to Stroud via another mill area in Lancashire; the others followed later. The reason for the migration is not explained, but it was probably economic. Stroud, with its flourishing cloth mills, was attracting migrants from the low employment areas of neighbouring counties and the south coast. Sail was giving way to steam, and the smaller harbours were losing trade.

The Lee brothers set up as shopkeepers in or near Stroud and did well. Howard Beard, a relative of Laurie's from a younger generation, has undertaken research on the family's history and commented: 'If they had not migrated here when they did, *Cider with Rosie* might have been set in Dorset and the book might have had quite a different title.'

Reginald Joseph arrived in Stroud as a schoolboy. After leaving school he quickly adapted to a new way of life in Gloucestershire and embarked on a series of occupations which led eventually, after the First World War, to a professional career in London. This was something many reasonably educated men from provincial homes aspired to in the 1920s, their horizons broadened by their wartime experiences. His father William's later years are something of a mystery: in the absence of clear evidence it seems possible that he left his family and returned to Bridport. A William Lee died there in 1897. Certainly Laurie never knew his paternal grandfather.

Reg married Katherine Critchley, daughter of a Brimscombe knitting-needle factory owner. She was said to be strikingly beautiful, and the family was well-to-do. Critchley's still exists as a factory by the canal near Stroud, but it no longer manufactures knitting-needles. Reg and Katherine had eight children, including twins who survived their mother by only a few weeks. She died in childbirth, aged thirty. The five children who survived into adulthood were Marjorie, Dorothy, Phyllis, Harold and Reggie – all except Reggie feature in *Cider with Rosie*.

By the time Annie Light arrived to work as Reg's housekeeper and to look after the children, whose ages ranged from twelve to three, he was studying for the Civil Service, determined to haul himself out of what he saw as the bourgeois world of Stroud trade. With Annie he had four children: Jack (christened Wilfred Jack Reginald) in 1912, Frances in 1913, Laurie in 1914 and Tony in 1916. Laurie was born two days after midsummer on 26 June 1914 and christened Laurence Edward Alan Lee – L.E.A. Lee. He never signed himself so, always plain Laurie Lee.

Almost immediately after Laurie's birth Reg volunteered for the Army Pay Corps and was posted to London, a major step in his career plan. He never returned permanently to his family, although he sent his children money on their birthdays and occasionally visited them. Annie, who always hoped he would rejoin her, set out to create a family home away from Stroud. She went house-hunting and caught the carrier's cart up the valley to Slad, half-way between Stroud and her old home at Sheepscombe. There she made a home for herself and her brood of three sons and four stepchildren. One stepson, Reggie, stayed in Stroud with his Lee grandmother. Annie's only daughter, Frances, died soon after the move at the age of four and was buried in Slad churchyard.

When he was forty-five Laurie wrote his best-seller recalling – with Wordsworthian emotion recollected in tranquillity – the prelapsarian world of a child growing up in cheerful poverty and in the surprisingly happy security of what would now be termed a single-parent family. Their mother gave them all the warmth and affection the children could ask for. Laurie scarcely missed his absent father, and the older sisters seemed like extra mothers to him.

What is there in his background to throw light on the sources of his imaginative prose and impressionistic poems? His rare writing talent flowered when he was thirty and bloomed for more than forty years, ranging through prose, poetry and drama. A few clues exist here and there: a great-grandfather who sailed the world and perhaps handed down to his descendants a passion for travel; enterprising, adventurous males on both sides of the family, although none of them writers; a mother who captured her children's imaginations with fireside stories and lived at times in a world of fantasy. And, later, there was a schoolteacher who perceived an unusual boy and nurtured his talent and his enthusiasm for reading.

Laurie, as an adult, would say that the Cotswolds made him – 'the moods of the earth, seedtime and harvest, the great cycle of the seasons'. He was impelled to write partly by a fear that the words of his village story 'were being sung for the last time and were passing into perpetual silence'.[4] From then on everything he wrote seemed to look back to his village, his valley and the great sweep of landscape that lies between the river Severn and the Thames.

2
Through the Valley

I hear the sad rinsing of reeded meadows
The small lakes rise in the wild white rose
The shudder of wings in the streaming cedars
And tears of lime running down from the hills.
— 'Summer Rain'

To walk from Stroud to Sheepscombe is to walk through Laurie Lee's life. This is the valley carved out by the Slad Brook, which rises in Down Wood just south of Sheepscombe, wanders down through Slad and Uplands and finally joins the small river Frome in Stroud. The valley threads together the story of the Lights and the Lees.

Starting at the southern end of the valley, the first landmark is barely half a mile from the town centre in the steep suburb called Uplands. Here perched on banks facing the Slad Brook, in some cases backing on to it, is a series of small, late Victorian villas built between 1860 and 1880. One of these is Glenview.

A stone's throw further along is All Saints Church, where Reg Lee and Annie Light were married and their children were baptized. Here is a great stone barn of a place built in 1910 to replace an earlier church, but it remains undecorated – no colour, no stained glass, no wall tablets, just stone. Although it is now a suburb of Stroud, mainly built up in Victorian times, Uplands still retains the atmosphere of a village, with its church, post office and pub clustering just off the road to Slad.

The moderately busy road winds on uphill between disused mills and neat bungalows until the houses thin out and give way to green fields, as the valley gets wider and deeper. About two miles from Stroud is Gravel Hill House, where Lucie Godsell lived – she used to play piano in the Slad Players' Christmas pantomimes in which Laurie would participate as a boy – and just beyond it Woodside House, home of Dr Reginald Green, Stroud's medical officer of health whose wife used to produce the pantomimes each year.

Then comes The Vatch, a hamlet on both sides of the brook, which in Laurie's childhood still had a working mill. The converted millhouse and a partly medieval farmhouse are reminders of The Vatch's past. Cows being herded in for milking and sheepdogs rounding up flocks are a normal part of the valley scene between here and Slad.

Soon Slad comes into view: its handsome church spire and gilded clock show above a screen of trees, and Laurie's village spills down the valley side, not greatly changed since 1917. On the left, tucked below the churchyard, is the Old School with so many memories of his childhood, and on the right is the seventeenth-century Woolpack Inn, where the writer held court in his later years. Behind the Woolpack stands Rose Cottage, occupied by Laurie when he returned to Slad, and Little Court, where he lived his last thirty years.

A hundred yards further on a steep grass bank slopes down from the road to a solid greystone house. Grassy steps support a wooden sign with the name Rosebank, although when Laurie was a child it had no official name – locals called it Mother Lee's Cottage. Across the valley are fields of cows, scattered farms and an orchard which once grew cider apples.

Immediately behind Rosebank there is a glimpse of a cream-coloured mansion by a lake: this is Steanbridge House and its grounds, where all the major annual events in the village were held. The narrow lane down to Steanbridge and its millpond was once the village road, replaced now by the main road from Birdlip to Stroud. A deeply scooped hollow-way crossing Steanbridge Lane marks the old drovers' track from Painswick to Cirencester. The history of Slad as a settlement and a route junction is concentrated in a stone bridge over the Slad Brook at this point, too narrow to give passage to anything but animals and small carts.

The next landmark is the village war memorial, inscribed with family names linked to some of Laurie's schoolfellows. After this one continues on and up towards Bulls Cross, beneath an arch of beech trees planted, according to Laurie, by his uncles – as he often told newcomers. These giant beeches may well be a hundred years old. Then, at the head of the valley, Bulls Cross itself, a rather desolate three-way crossroads seven hundred feet up where, so he said, a gibbet once stood and a ghostly coach could be seen on winter nights.

At this point the road to Painswick turns sharp left and the way to Sheepscombe swings half left along Longridge, where members of Laurie's family lived before he was born and younger members still do. Another mile or two, passing by hamlets called Cockshoot and Jack's Green, the walker reaches the outskirts of Sheepscombe with its attractive Methodist chapel and church built in the nineteenth century by its tiny community and – standing on its own – a limewashed building with the remains of a inn sign. Its name: the Plough, once the home of Laurie's mother, her father and her five brothers.

A short walk downhill into Sheepscombe village leads to the Butchers' Arms, where Lights and Lees gathered for beer after village cricket matches; and high up behind the pub is the village pitch, which used to be on private land until Laurie bought it for Sheepscombe in perpetuity.

Laurie Lee is not the only writer to have immortalized this particular corner of Gloucestershire. C. Henry Warren, a London journalist, later to be deputy editor of the *Radio Times*, migrated to the south Cotswolds in 1932 and left a record of his affection for the area in *A Cotswold Year*, published in 1936. He also wrote *England Is a Village* and articles for *Country Life*.

Warren's cottage was at Woodend, on the western edge of the Cotswolds looking across to the river Severn but within walking distance of Painswick. Sheepscombe particularly appealed to him: 'A spirit of independence seems to characterize all the activities of . . . Sheepscombe, a little community in the hills surrounding Painswick . . . There was never a squire in Sheepscombe, hence their self-reliance.' And he repeated the often told account of the Painswick parson's wife who inspired Sheepscombers to build their own church at night, working by moonlight and by lantern after toiling all day.[1]

At about the same time that he found himself in Sheepscombe, Warren discovered Miserden. It was a dark night just before Christmas, he reported, and the village seemed deserted – he correctly guessed that all the men were in the Carpenters' Arms. He walked into a 'smoke-dense room' with oil lamps, a wood fire with steel spits and saw about thirty men singing folk songs 'to the impromptu accompaniment of the fiddler, who wandered in and out among the singing crowd, shutting his eyes and sweeping his bow up to the ceiling'. There were solos, choruses and ballads and 'a masterly performance of "The Barley Mow" . . . I do not know a more attractive inn anywhere in the Cotswolds,' Warren concluded. He was writing this around 1933, when Laurie was nineteen and spending a considerable amount of time playing the violin and reading poetry in local pubs shortly before he set off on his travels. Miserden was one of his favourite haunts and it is possible that it was he who was fiddling at the Carpenters' Arms.

Another coincidence: on a ramble along the towpath of the Stroudwater Canal at Brimscombe Warren came across some mills whose 'faded lettering announces the manufacture of hairpins and knitting needles and so forth'. This must have been Critchley's Pin Mill, where Reg Lee wooed the owner's daughter nearly forty years before and where his son Reg junior later became a director.

The Cotswolds in the 1930s were relatively unknown to city dwellers and tourists. With the exception of some people involved in the Arts and Crafts movement, the Whiteway Colonists and a few writers – among them John Masefield and W.H. Davies – very few intellectuals had colonized the area. Villages such as Slad and Miserden kept their identity intact; few people moved into them and few moved away, unless perhaps to find work. In the 1930s mains water, electricity and indoor sanitation were still largely unknown in rural areas. The commuters, the weekenders and the holiday cottage tenants did not arrive until after the Second World War, bringing with them cars, television and telephones. Warren discovered, and Laurie knew, an almost feudal way of life. Laurie was to write that his was the last generation to live as country people had done for centuries. Radical changes were not far away.

Warren watched a man ploughing with a team of shire horses, another one making a drystone wall and others cutting wood. He talked to locals about the Mop Fairs, where farmworkers and servants looking for employment lined up with a badge on their coats to show their trade. It was so called because the housemaids would parade with mops. He listened to nightingales and watched beekeepers collecting honey.[2] Had he but known it, the war was to change the slow pace of country life for ever, and Laurie would be the one to record these changes most eloquently.

Laurie and Henry Warren were not the only writers who developed a deep and lasting affection for the Cotswolds early in the century. Ivor Gurney, the composer-poet born in Gloucester, yearned to be on Birdlip and Crickley Hills in the poems he wrote as a private soldier in the First World War. P.J. Kavanagh, who edited Gurney's collected poems in 1984, felt that it was misleading to call him a local poet – his Gloucestershire was 'a region of the mind'.

After the war, when he was battling against mental illness, Gurney drew immense comfort from walking the Cotswold hills. He sent many letters to Marion Scott, a friend from his days at the Royal College of Music who transcribed his compositions and poems. In autumn 1916 he wrote from the trenches: 'How the leaves must be flying on Cranham . . . Painswick Beacon will stand as high and immovable as ever . . . O for the wild woods and the leaves flying!'[3]

In 1919 he marvelled at the steepness of Birdlip Hill, where 'even the Romans crooked the road'; later he walked at dawn on Crickley Hill, where 'the woods were calm and pierced through with stars of the quietest'. One of his last poems spoke of 'Cotswolds glorifying God'. Ivor Gurney and Laurie Lee were a generation apart, yet born within four or five miles of each other and drawing inspiration from the same few square miles of hills, streams and woods.

Another writer who walked hundreds of miles across the Cotswolds was Norman Jewson, the Arts and Crafts architect. Jewson came by train to Cirencester in 1907, aged twenty-three, and enterprisingly hired a donkey and cart for a camping and sketching holiday. In Sapperton, on the edge of Cirencester Park, he met his hero, the architect-craftsman Ernest Gimson, and the Barnsley brothers, gurus of the Arts and Crafts movement. Gimson invited Jewson to work for him, and a chance holiday turned into a 68-year residence. He worked on or restored famous Cotswold manor houses, among them Owlpen. He lived at Frampton Mansell, Oakridge and eventually Sapperton and walked to every village within a ten-mile radius. His book, *By Chance I Did Rove,* describes in loving detail each community, its legends, characters and occupations.

All of these villages would have been familiar to Laurie, lying as they did between Slad and Cirencester, and he may well have read Jewson's book when it was published in 1951. Since Jewson lived until 1975 they may even have met – Slad and Sapperton were barely ten miles apart.

All four writers were inspired by the same south Cotswold land-scape in the 1920s, although Laurie and Jewson wrote about it years later. Laurie summed up the appeal of the place: 'I belonged to that generation which saw, by chance, the end of a thousand years' life . . . born in a world of silence, a world of hard work and necessary patience . . . the horse was king . . . Then, to the scream of the horse, the change began. The brass-lamped motor car came coughing up the road.' The poets, the journalist and the architect were recording a unique aspect of social history: rural life in the Gloucestershire Cotswolds before the coming of the car.

3

Birthplace: Stroud

On eves of cold, when slow coal fires,
rooted in basements, burn and branch,
brushing with smoke the city air . . .
Above the muffled traffic then
I hear the owl.

– 'Town Owl'

T HE Stroud Laurie Lee was born into in 1914 was a busy mill town bisected by a river, a railway and a canal. The town straggles along the narrow valley of the river Frome. Five steep valleys clamber up, like the outstretched fingers of a hand, on to the limestone Cotswold hills.

On the other side of the Severn lies Wales, linked to most of Gloucestershire in 1914 only by the rail tunnel beneath the river to Bristol, one of Isambard Kingdom Brunel's great engineering projects. Years later a mile-long road bridge would span the Severn, but before the First World War the nearest practical crossing for cattle drovers and early motorists was a dozen miles away, at Gloucester. Later still, when a second road bridge was under construction, Laurie told an interviewer: 'We live close to our origins here. I love the feeling of being right on the edge of Cotswold history, with the Severn as our defence against the barbarians.'[1]

Forty miles from the seaport of Bristol, a hundred miles from London, Stroud was relatively isolated before the Great War. The railway was its chief lifeline, and this made Stroud Station an important focus of activity. Trade on the canal was declining, but narrow boats still shifted coal, hay and timber from the docks at Sharpness to the river Thames beyond Cirencester. Mechanical road traffic was slowly displacing the horse: there were more and more motor buses, commercial vehicles and charabancs.

It was the mills that made Stroud; at first cloth mills, depending on

Cotswold wool and the fast, clean water of the valleys, then engine-driven mills, turning out all kinds of products. By 1914 the population of greater Stroud reached about seven thousand, working in the mills, in farming, on the canal or the railway. In the whole area there were eighty-seven mills, and locals boasted that Stroud could produce anything from a pin to a steam engine.

Impressive country houses were built on the outskirts by the wealthy mill and factory owners, and terraced rows of red-brick cottages sprang up to accommodate the workers. Terraces grew up all over the steep valley sides, alongside the railway and out towards neighbouring towns. It was Stroud's reputation as a mill town that brought in migrants such as the Lee family. When the Bridport Lees arrived near the end of Queen Victoria's reign Stroud was already well equipped with shops, factories, offices and small red-brick villas. It was in one of these that William and Emma Lee settled around 1891.

Reg and Katherine Lee set up their own home on the outskirts of Stroud, in Uplands, in Edward VII's reign. After his young wife's death and his marriage to Annie Reg transferred his growing family from Uplands Road to Glenview, which was slightly larger and round the corner in the Slad Road. Nevertheless they kept in close touch with their former next-door neighbours, the Chapman family.

Vera Chapman, a retired schoolteacher, was born just four months before Laurie. She recalled that her mother Alice assisted at the births of some of the Lees and that two of Laurie's stepsisters did occasional duty as babysitters for the Chapmans. Vera Chapman was little more than a baby when the Lees moved away from Uplands Road, but she remembered them well. 'My older brother Reg showed one of the young Lees how to ride a bike, and later on, when I was at the High School, a friend lent her bike to one of the boys. Perhaps it was Laurie or Tony.' After the move to Slad Annie Lee maintained her friendship with Vera Chapman's mother, calling on her from time to time. 'I used to play the piano, and Mrs Lee liked to sing. The song I particularly remember was "O don't deceive me, O never leave me! How could you use a poor maiden so?" Of course I had no idea at the time how appropriate it was. She was a lovely person, a scatterbrain, and Laurie brings out her character in many ways in *Cider with Rosie*.'

The local newspaper published on the day of Laurie's birth in June 1914 records no momentous events. There had been a fatal motor-cycle accident near Painswick – unusual in those days – and a Brims-combe man had drowned in the canal. The Nailsworth branch of the National Union of Women's Suffrage Societies met at Horsley Priory that month; the suffragette campaign was nearing its climax, and reports suggest that it had a good many supporters in the Stroud area among middle-class women and mill workers. The paper was full of summer sales notices. Bedsteads could be picked up for ten shillings in the Co-op shop (Laurie recalled his mother freewheeling on her bicycle downhill without brakes to the store, failing to stop and having to be caught by a nimble shop assistant). Cows with their calves fetched £27 at Gloucester Cattle Market, and an Ebley man won six prizes for cider at Cheltenham Agricultural Show. Many cider apple orchards added charm to the valleys around Stroud. Gloucester Old Spot pigs, often fed in the same orchards, would have done well at the market too.

That week's *Stroud News* conveys a picture of warm, sleepy south Gloucestershire. Yet only a week later parish pump news gave way to an ominous headline: 'Assassination of the Austrian Heir'.

By 14 August, after war had been declared, the *Stroud News* adver-tisements reflected the sombre mood of the country. A recruiting notice declared: 'Your Country Needs You – 10,000 Men Needed Immediately – God Save the King!' And a local shirtmaker appealed to his customers to make bandages: 'How Can We Help Our Soldiers and Sailors?'

Stroud had its share of poverty and unemployment. The Work-house, outwardly a not unattractive brick building on Eastington Hill, filled up each winter with the destitute: Laurie's story of the aged Slad couple, Joseph and Hannah Brown, who were transferred to the Workhouse to die, still strikes a chord among elderly readers. The Army offered a way to escape the poverty trap and a chance of social advancement. Those local men who had fought in India or South Africa and survived returned home as heroes and role models for their younger brothers. When recruiting began in earnest for this new war there was a wave of patriotic enthusiasm.

The Gloucestershire Regiment had its barracks in Gloucester, but all over the county towns raised militia and territorial units. They paraded with bands playing, setting up recruitment depots in market-places and village halls. In the first week thirty men joined up from the village of Painswick. In some places a whole generation of local men went to war. They fought in the trenches and died side by side.

Stroud was not short of volunteers. Crowds gathered at the station to watch the first troop trains pull out (taking men of the Fifth Gloucesters to training camps on the Isle of Wight), and Cotswold farmers brought their horses down from the hills to sell them in the station yard to the Army. They were used as cavalry mounts, as baggage ponies and to draw gun carriages. Few horses ever came back from France.

Reg Lee was one Stroud man among many who volunteered, seeing it as a step on his way to a professional career and away from the Co-op. Much later Laurie laughed about his father wearing a bullet-proof jacket, although he was only a Pay Corps clerk at Greenwich: 'It was a very stout piece of equipment, like the quilt they strap on horses in a bullfight. He developed a very peculiar walk as a result. Dear Dad, he was a bit of a joke really.'[2] Later on Laurie's headmaster had to sign an Army pension form stating that the boy's father was incapacitated through war service. Annie said that the incapacity was due to nerves.

The coming of war impinged little on the life of a baby, but times were not easy for young mothers during this period. Many felt pressure to undertake war work. Several Stroud mills changed over from cloth-making to munitions, and women filled the place of men as they joined the forces. For the first time ever, women who had previously seen no openings beyond domestic service were employed in factories. They also helped out in the breweries, in the factories manufacturing walking-sticks and umbrellas and in the pin mills.

Other jobs were available in Stroud Hospital, opened in 1875, as well as the post office, shops and offices. But this liberation from domestic drudgery was not for Annie, with four children of school age and three toddlers to look after. Wartime families were exhorted to 'tighten their belts', and there were food shortages and constant appeals for comforts for men at the front. Like many women, Annie knitted socks for the British soldiers. Apart from this, her days were filled mainly with finding food and preparing it for the seven children, bathing them in a tin hipbath, sewing and mending and other domestic chores. She boiled their clothes in a copper, mangled them dry and ironed them with a flat-iron. It was tedious, repetitive work for an intelligent woman of spirit and imagination.

Annie found town life oppressive and missed the sense of community she had experienced in the village. Sometimes she would catch a bus up the valley to visit her ageing father at Sheepscombe or the wives of some of her brothers who had settled in the Painswick area. All of them, like her, had husbands away at the war. She envied their less housebound way of life and longed to escape from Stroud. The town had some entertainment to offer – by 1914 there were two cinemas, the Empire and the Picture House, as well as the Subscription Rooms for public meetings, a free library with over six thousand books and a dance hall – but only the library would have been accessible to Annie, given her circumstances.

A weekly treat for the family was a visit to Reg's mother's shop at Wallbridge, by the canal. Here she sold fruit and vegetables, sweets and tobacco and would hand out liquorice sticks and aniseed balls to her grandchildren. A photograph from that time shows a homely woman in black holding a kitten and standing by a shop window ('Lee, Greengrocery and Confectionery') advertising Cadbury's Chocolate, Westward Ho! Smoking Mixture and Fry's Pure Tobacco. This was Emma Lee, who had migrated with her family from Dorset and in widowhood, or possibly after her husband's disappearance, managed the shop that William had once run.

Life in wartime Stroud could not have been an ideal environment for a toddler to grow up in: noisy, smoke-filled and filthy underfoot. The town echoed to the hiss and bustle of railway engines, the clattering of factory machinery and mill looms, the piercing hooters of factories and trains. And there was always horse traffic. Mud and dung littered the roads. Every building was blackened by smoke. Tuberculosis and influenza were common infant killers (three of Reg's children had died soon after birth, one more would die as a small child). Laurie described himself as a sickly baby who was not expected to live; yet a picture of him aged about five shows a chubby-cheeked, normal-looking boy.

The family at Glenview may have suffered less than most from pollution and dirty streets, living some distance uphill from the town centre. The smaller children could play safely in the villa's tiny garden and hunt for tadpoles in the relatively clean waters of the Slad brook opposite the house. The children knew how to entertain themselves. They could watch the huge engines rumbling over Brunel's handsome eleven-arch railway viaduct and play by the Stroudwater Canal, where heavily laden narrow boats would slide past pulled by massive shire horses or legged by men through the tunnels. There was also the annual Agricultural and Horticultural Show, when the whole town was decked out with flags, bunting and floral arches. And small boys could, of course, occupy their free time playing marbles, fishing for tiddlers or, more occasionally, watching travelling Punch and Judy shows. Laurie's older brothers, Harold and Jack, as Sunday School attenders, may have gone on the annual outing by charabanc to Weston-super-Mare or the Cheddar Caves.

Laurie's chief childhood memory of his father was a photograph of a stranger 'with a badged cap and a spiked moustache'. For many children of his generation it was the only memory of their fathers they would ever have. With an energetic mother and a warm, loving family Laurie is unlikely to have missed his absent father, and he would hardly have been aware of any social deprivation. In any case he was soon to start a new life in a different place.

4
Slad Days

If ever I saw blessing in the air
I see it now in this still early day
Where lemon-green the vaporous morning drips
Wet sunlight on the powder of my eye
                                        – 'April Rise'

To Laurie aged three, Slad seemed a paradise on earth. The reality was rather less idyllic. In 1917 the village with its satellite hamlets had a population of about 250, most of them living in cottages with no modern facilities: no electricity, no indoor lavatory, no piped water, no bathroom. The public buildings consisted of a church with a two-room school alongside, both built in the mid nineteenth century, a Congregational chapel and two inns – a third had disappeared. The church had a substantial vicarage and the chapel a manse.

Apart from the owners of the part-Georgian Steanbridge House (called the Big House by Laurie), only four other people figured in Slad's list of private residents: two maiden ladies, the Misses Bagnall, Mr Horace Webb at Knapp Farm and the Stroud medical officer of health, Dr Reginald Green. The village had six farmers, a coachman, three gardeners, a builder and a boot repairer, as well as the two innkeepers and Mr George Vick who ran the post office shop. Local men worked mainly in farming or at one of the nearby factories – the Pin Mill at Painswick, the Woodlands Cloth Mill at Slad or the Hound Brand Tailoring Factory on the road to Stroud.[1]

The village was not entirely isolated, for a carrier's cart called each day at four o'clock on its way from Stroud to Sheepscombe. But for most Slad people the village might as well have had a fortress wall; they were self-sufficient except for a baker, a dairyman and a fish-monger who called. Most people grew vegetables and fruit and kept hens; they cut wood for fires and kept a stock of lamp-oil and candles, for at least once every winter they were cut off by heavy snowfall. Painswick, Sheepscombe and Uplands were considered an easy walk away, and for those who had to get into Stroud regularly an infrequent bus service started up a year or two after the Lees moved to Slad.

Eighty years later Slad has not changed much superficially – apart from the constant through traffic. These days villagers commute to work further afield, in Cheltenham, Gloucester and Bristol, but Slad is still recognizably the virtually one-street village the Lees moved to in 1917. Even though the chapel is now a bed-and-breakfast establishment and the post office, vicarage, manse, school and Star Inn have become private houses, Laurie's old home – now called Rosebank – has kept its character and appearance (if not its name). Nowadays the village has no shop, but there is still an occasional bus service.

Family life at the Lees' cottage was a saga of making ends meet, getting by somehow, surviving the harsh winters and the annual flooding. It was a time of deadly influenza epidemics and children's ailments which often proved fatal. Laurie was very ill as an infant and again when he was about four, apparently with pneumonia. He survived against the odds; but his much-loved sister Frances, Annie Lee's only daughter, died at the age of four, possibly from tuberculosis. Many of the smaller gravestones in Slad churchyard, some dating from as late as the 1930s, record child and infant mortality.

Laurie started school when he was four years old and at first found it traumatic after the carefree existence of a cherished son who slept in his mother's bed, was cosseted by older sisters and played fantasy games in the fields and woods of the Slad Valley. But he was an adaptable, easy-going child and he soon took school in his stride.

Slad School's logbook, scrupulously kept by successive head-teachers, reveals that there were over a hundred pupils on the roll at the time – they came from neighbouring hamlets and up the valley – but attendance averaged just sixty-five because of bad weather, illness or because of parents' need to eke out inadequate family incomes by getting their children to do casual work on farms or in the mills. They were taught in two groups, Infants and Big Room, by the headteacher and two unqualified young assistants.[2]

One cannot be sure how accurate Laurie's memories of Slad School were when he described it in *Cider with Rosie* forty years later. Some names are authentic, some not. Miss Ethel Hedden was the headmistress from 1916 to 1920, so she must have been 'Crabby B', by his account not well liked. He names Miss Patience Wardley, who succeeded her, but not the various assistants who came and went: Phyllis King, Mrs Vick (wife of the postmaster?), Miss Foulds, Marjorie Lawson, Nesta Dunham, Dorothy Cratchley. Perhaps they fused in Laurie's mind as one warm, caring person who made up for the sternness of headmistresses.

Then there were his fellow scholars. He mentioned his brothers – Jack was the genius of the family, he said, Tony an imaginative nonconformist who did his own thing. No Jack Lee appears in the school logbook for the years 1917–24, but there is a Wilfred R. Lee who was caned once for persistent talking. Evidently he was Jack at home but Wilfred at school.

Some names occur both in the logbook and in Laurie's memoirs: Walter Kerry, Fred and Poppy Green, Betty Gleed. Then there was Jim Fern, an exact contemporary of Tony. When they started school together big brother Laurie used to escort them across the road. Seventy-five years later Jim was living in Stroud and leading guided walks around his old schoolfellow's domain. He, too, wrote a book about his Slad childhood, entitled *Ferns in the Valley*.

Miss Hedden ran a tight ship and did her best to keep the school going in the face of absenteeism by staff and children alike. Sometimes the school was given permission by the Stroud Education Board to close because of heavy snowfalls or an epidemic of whooping cough, chicken pox or influenza. All of these could be killers. Once or twice the school had to shut when coal was not delivered for its single stove.

But when the children were fit, the weather fine and food and fuel plentiful, there was much to feed their imaginations too. One thing they did not go short of was books. In one term sixty *Globe Poetry Books*, twelve copies of *World's Childhood*, thirty-six *Treasure Trove Story* readers and twenty-four *Bright Story* readers were delivered. A circulating library box arrived regularly from Gloucester, and pupils learned to sing hymns and recite Bible stories by heart. The Vicar of Slad came to examine them, and on one visit he reported that 'the infants knew nearly all the words'.

The First World War is mentioned only briefly in the logbook, yet it cast a huge shadow over staff and students. Mrs Vick, Miss Hedden's first assistant, was away from time to time either because her husband was on leave or was about to return to the war. Gardening was introduced as a new weekly subject – and a popular one – justified by the need to grow more food. Slad Food Production Society leased twenty-two perches of allotment land to the school, and tools and seeds were supplied. The chief crop for several years was potatoes.

In 1917 a lecture was given to the children on 'the Inadvertent Disclosure of Military Information'. What military secrets could these rural schoolchildren have given away? Movements of troop trains, perhaps, or horse-drawn Army wagons trundling through the lanes.

Then on 11 November 1918 the Vicar came to the school unexpectedly to announce that the Armistice had been signed. After four years of war the children could hardly understand what this meant. The logbook records: 'We had the National Anthem, and cheers for King, Empire, Allies – and soldiers and sailors.' And later in the week: 'Several lessons were devoted to talking about the great news.'

The four-year-old Laurie must have wondered when his long-gone father would return. Some children's fathers or uncles never returned. The Slad War Memorial carries names familiar from Laurie's memoirs – Bullock, Fern, Hogg, Robinson. For Annie the news revived her hope that Reg would rejoin his family, but after demobilization he joined the Civil Service and settled in London. Laurie professed not to miss his father, the man in uniform with a spiked moustache. Certainly there was nothing in his later writing to suggest any profound psychological effect from growing up in a one-parent family.

Laurie painted a picture of his father as rather a dashing cavalier. It might be nearer the mark to perceive a sentimental man, nominally attached to his large family – but always from a distance. His letters suggest someone reasonably well educated, conscious of appearances, self-important. In 1917, after the death of Frances, he wrote to Annie from his army billet in Woolwich:

Dear Nance,

Thanks for wire. God's will be done. May he help us to bear our sorrow and our bereavement. May our little darling be evergreen in our memory and a shining light to us till we are again reunited.

O, how she must have suffered at the last, poor little dearie, Dad's little Bluebell. Don't worry and fret, old girl – I wish I were near to try to console you. Take Baby Tony out in the pram. I will come if I can but I don't think they will extend my leave.

. . . Order a wreath from [a florist] for you and I, and another for the children. I will pay for these.

With love to all, your affectionate husband in sorrow,

Reg [3]

This may have been simulated grief; he apparently did not get to Slad for the funeral. It may be that he had already decided not to return to the family home. Jack remembered his father as 'artistic in the sense that he was a good musician, otherwise somewhat mean and pedantic . . . he was a cold man'. Laurie recorded that Reg sent £1 each week to Annie with a note: 'Dear Nance, Herewith the usual.' On the whole his visits to the Stroud area were limited to weddings and twenty-first birthday parties.

After the war the older boys at Slad School played football, a new school activity, and a field was rented for sport. Piped water came to the village, one tap per household, and some families, although not the Lees, exchanged their draughty outdoor privies for less chilly ones tacked on to their houses.

In 1922 another innovation in the school curriculum was introduced, one that appealed to Laurie more than football: a travelling violin teacher visited once a week to give lessons. Years later Laurie recalled that a violin belonging to his father had hung on the wall in the Uplands house. In time he inherited it, and his father was prevailed upon to pay for a bow to go with it. He was a fast learner, and quite soon Laurie with his fiddle was in demand for church teas and parish events. His first public performance, aged about ten, was with a local girl pianist, Eileen Brown. Together they played the 'Poet and Peasant Overture' and 'Danny Boy', and to their surprise the audience joined in singing. 'Danny Boy' was later to prove a useful source of income in his busking days. Those first few party pieces were the beginning of a lifelong attachment to the violin, carried to and played in many countries. His first fiddle, he claimed, was eventually crushed by a bull in Málaga.

In a television programme filmed for his eightieth birthday, Laurie recalled the excitement of setting up a three-piece village dance band called the Three Blind Mice. He played the fiddle, a beekeeper played the drums and a cobbler from Stroud was on the piano. Weekly dances were the high spot of rural teenage society in the 1920s, and the Three Blind Mice were paid five shillings a dance and were given free lemonade.

Another local entertainment involving the whole Lee family took place at Christmas 1925, when Laurie was eleven. This was the pantomime *Cinderella,* presented at Slad Schoolroom by the light of oil lamps, the first major production of the newly formed Slad Players, directed by Mrs Kirsty Green, the doctor's wife.

Michael Holloway of Box, born in Stroud in 1913, played the drums for the pantomime with his maiden aunt, Miss Lucie Godsell, on piano. The Godsells were well-known local brewers, and Lucie, who had studied music in Paris, lived with her mother at Gravel Hill, on the edge of Slad. She gave her nephew his first drum kit and suggested that he might like to gain experience by helping out the Slad Players – he had taught himself mainly by listening to gramophone records. He recalled: 'We played "Yes, Sir, That's My Baby" and other popular tunes. The Lee family were very involved with the pantomime. Marjorie was a beautiful Cinderella; Dorothy, the dark one, was Prince Charming and Phyl was Dandini. Laurie was too young to act, so he sold programmes for a penny or tuppence a time. They were handwritten by the schoolchildren. I don't think he played his violin in that show. We did *Cinderella* three times, as far as I can recall, and another panto the next year. After that Mrs Green put on Noel Coward and Ian Hay comedies at the old Empire in Stroud.'[4]

He kept up his drumming as a medical student in London and went on to practise medicine in London, returning to Stroud for holidays. He remembered seeing Marjorie working in a shop in Russell Street and said she still looked very lovely. He was not to meet Laurie again until the 1970s: 'I asked him if he would agree to be president of the Cotswold Players, and he did that for two or three years. We were all terribly interested when *Cider with Rosie* came out. Later I talked to Laurie about the *Cider with Rosie* film. He said he didn't have much to do with it.'

Michael Holloway returned to live at Box, close to Stroud, in his retirement and bought a house not far from where Marjorie lived until her death in 1994 at the age of ninety-one.

Other members of Laurie's family, too, have memories of Slad in the 1920s. Charlie Light, born in 1913 and the oldest of Laurie's cousins, remembered him best at cricket matches. Charlie was a forester all his working life, as was his father Charles, and Laurie was proud to tell people that the family of his uncle Charles had planted many of Gloucestershire's finest estate beechwoods – among them Painswick, Cirencester, Kingscote and Rendcomb. Those sapling trees planted after the First World War are now giants, dominating the landscape and featuring in some of Laurie's poems.

Charlie was born at Sheepscombe in a cottage behind the Butchers' Arms, where he lived until he left school in 1927. Then he moved to Rendcomb with his parents Charles and Fanny, his sisters Joan and Edith and his brother Ray. 'Auntie Annie used to bring the boys up from the cottage at Slad to see us, but it was always so late when they arrived they had to walk home in the dark. I knew Jack best – he was nearest to my age. He was pretty smart, and he and Laurie were much brighter than the rest of us boys. They had a different way of talking. I think there may be something in Laurie's idea that Auntie Annie was descended from a mysterious person in the Light family.' Another of Charlie's memories was of several cousins riding on a carrier's cart – the same cart that first deposited Laurie at the age of three in Slad – to visit an aunt in Cheltenham. 'It was terribly cold going down Leckhampton Hill. We stopped to warm ourselves at a road mender's brazier.'

Frances and Marion Light, daughters of Annie's brother Sid, born in 1921 and 1923 respectively, laughed when they recalled the cottage in Slad. 'We loved walking down to Slad. Mother would warn us not to bring any of Annie's junk back. She collected everything. She'd buy a Spode teapot at a sale even if it had three rivets in the lid, and she'd give us pieces of china too. There were flowers everywhere – the garden was a wilderness and she'd bring in great bunches so that you could hardly see her behind them.'

Frances and Marion were born in the hamlet of Longridge, halfway between Slad and Sheepscombe, and moved back to their childhood home when they retired to a cottage within a mile or two of the Plough. Like other members of the clan they went away but eventually gravitated back to their roots. 'Auntie Annie was so scatterbrained,' said Marion. 'I have a Sunday school prize Bible of hers with a letter in it she wrote to Laurie but never sent. She said: "Where are you now? I always knew where you were when you were a little boy, but now you're Laurie Lee, poet and writer, I can't see you."'

The Light family also recalled Laurie at cricket matches. 'We would cycle to matches with our father, maybe over to Cranham or Duntisbourne Abbots. Laurie used to watch, but he did not play. Jack was a fine cricketer, and after he left home he'd bring teams down from London to play at Sheepscombe. Then everyone would get together in the Butchers' Arms.' Laurie's violin-playing was a familiar sound to Frances and Marion. 'They'd give little concerts, Leslie Workman on the drums, Harold Eyles at the piano and Laurie with his violin.'

The sisters' home is full of family photographs. A rare one featuring the whole of Annie's family shows a happy-looking Reg, tall and balding, at the wedding of his middle daughter Dorothy to Leslie Robinson. Annie is there, too, as the bride's stepmother, in a large black hat with feathers, standing at some distance from her husband. Marjorie and Phyllis were bridesmaids, and the three brothers, fair-haired Jack, long-faced Laurie and dark Tony, are sitting on the ground in front.

By the end of the 1990s there were four generations of Lights living in the Stroud–Painswick area, a total of some fifteen survivors, with a few more scattered in Australia, Canada, London, Buckinghamshire and Northamptonshire. If they were all alive now the six children of Frances Light and John would have twenty-four descendants. This is the family who with their ancestors are pictured in *Cider with Rosie*.

Another family member who remembers Reg vividly is Diana Roper, born in 1928, daughter of Reg's oldest daughter Marjorie. 'When my grandfather was a Civil Servant he used to visit us in Rodborough, and he always gave two and sixpence and chocolate silver pennies to my foster-brother John and me. He was tall, with Churchill-type hair strained across and a diamond tie-pin. I remember that he scratched his initials on one of our windows. We only saw him once or twice a year, but he was always interested in what his grandchildren were doing.' Marjorie trained as a milliner in Stroud and married Maurice Herbert in 1927 when she was twenty-four. Marjorie remained a beauty into her old age. 'She was tall, with wonderful long legs and marvellous bone structure and skin. Everyone said how beautiful she was,' Diana told me.

A year or two later Reg gave away his third daughter, Phyllis, to Harold Eyles. He was the amateur pianist who sometimes played in bands with Laurie and came from a well-known local family.

Another amateur musician who played with Laurie in the 1920s was Arthur Swain of Painswick, born in 1912, a friend of Laurie's brother Jack and Harold Eyles. Harold introduced Laurie to Arthur and they practised together in a room at the back of the former White Horse pub in Painswick, which was owned by Arthur's parents. Arthur recalled: 'Our place was like a second home to Laurie, and he often came for a meal. We started a little band called The Blue Rhythm and played dance tunes and Oscar Peterson-type music with another lad on the sax and one on the drums. We played at a few local dances for about a pound a night.'

He was an apprentice carpenter and Laurie had just left school, already with a bit of a reputation as a lady-killer. One of his girl-friends was Arthur's cousin Betty Smart (later Mrs Farmer), born in 1916.

She used to come over from Gloucester with her two sisters in the school holidays and stay with the Swain family; the three Smart girls and the three Lee boys were of similar age. 'Laurie was a very nice lad,' said Arthur. 'He would walk over from Slad and have a meal with us whenever he wanted, and we liked his mother, too.' The White Horse is no longer a pub, but Arthur, now in his late eighties, lives almost next door – and he still plays jazz.

Apart from playing the violin Laurie also sang in the church choir. The choristers had to attend weekly practice and two services on Sundays, in all weathers. At Christmas they sang carols round the village, but individual enterprise for pocket money was discouraged. Instead, their rewards were choir outings to the seaside or parties in the Squire's garden at Steanbridge.

Steanbridge House, an impressive mansion with lawns sweeping down to a lake and a cluster of farm buildings, was the social centre of Slad in the absence of a village hall. A wooden hut in the village was used by the Women's Institute and the Scouts, but all the major events in the year were held at Gilbert Jones's house.

Squire Jones was a well-to-do landowner, a civil engineer by profession, who acted as paterfamilias to the whole of Slad. Jim Fern said he remembered the entire village turning out for the Squire's funeral, with a carriage drawn by four black-plumed horses and the church bell tolling the years of the old man's life. A keen churchwarden, Grand Master of a benefit society and secretary of the local branch of the Tariff Reform League, the Squire threw open his grounds for fêtes, May Day entertainments and the annual Bird and Tree Festival, which included a half-day celebration at the house, with play-acting on the lawn, recitations, speeches by the Vicar and Mr Jones and a massive tea in the big barn.

The Bird and Tree Society, well documented in the school logbook, was set up to encourage natural history studies. Trees were planted and essays written in competition for a silver shield, which Slad School won more than once. A day was set aside for writing the essays, an exercise taken extremely seriously by the whole school. Laurie won a medal for an essay on otters. He admitted later to having culled the information from a book – it is certainly doubtful that he would have spotted otters in the Slad brook. In a film interview to commemorate his eightieth birthday he mentioned producing another essay on dabchicks, confessing that he would not have recognized one if he had seen one.

The school had other holidays: for Stroud Hospital Carnival, for Empire Day on 24 May (when the children were marched to church to sing patriotic songs and salute the Union Jack) and each autumn for the annual ritual of blackberry picking. Families like the Lees would never miss what was regarded as the free harvest of fields and hedges – mushrooms, rosehips and elderberries (the latter good for wine), sloes for making sloe gin and blackberries for jam and jelly.

Laurie does not seem to have drawn much attention to himself at the village school. Unlike his brother Jack he did not get caned for talking. He later said that he was content to sit at the back, do what he was told and wait for the bell. This seems out of character for one with the playful sense of humour and mischief he displayed in his writings, and out of school he certainly joined the village lads in whatever they were up to.

He read voraciously. In a collection of essays published in 1973 he recalls his mother reading aloud from Penny Readers, the only really cheap books that the literate working classes could obtain. The stories consisted of a mixture of sentimental morality and improbably dramatic plots. Laurie later recalled one story of a footman who rose to become a butler by thrift and prayer and another of a black boy who died in a fire to save his employer.[5]

After a year or two at school he graduated to reading *Pilgrim's Progress*, *Robinson Crusoe* and *Gulliver's Travels*, all 'improving' and good literature. Later still, returning from school in Stroud, he would visit Woolworth's or the local bookshop and browse through their Westerns and thrillers. He could get through their entire stock of books in a year, he said later. Either their stock was very small or he was a remarkable reader. It is obvious that reading played a large part in his life from an early age.

In 1925 he was one of three boys who left Slad School for the tougher discipline and harsher world of Stroud Central School for Boys. Many people have wondered why he did not follow his brother Jack to the local grammar school, the Marling, where Jack had passed the entrance examination. It is possible that their mother felt that Laurie might be overshadowed by Jack or that grammar school pressures were not for her younger son. His own explanation was: 'Oh, I was a lazy little beggar in those days.'

5
Stroud and Beyond

Where from the edge of day I spring
Alive for mortal flight
Lit by the heart's exploding sun
Bursting from night to night.

– 'The Edge of Day'

THE Stroud of Laurie's secondary school days was a lively, bustling town. The cloth mills flourished once more after the end of the First World War and new industries had started up, mainly in light engineering. As the Arts and Crafts movement grew, so the valleys became home to a wave of artistic, musical and literary figures – and this is still true of Stroud at the end of the century.

With a population of about 7,000, signs of prosperity began to appear in the town. By 1922 there were cars for some of the more affluent families (among them Gilbert Jones of Steanbridge House), telephones, a network of bus services linking the five valleys, several good schools, a public swimming pool and Turkish baths. Electricity, too, had arrived, bringing street lighting as well as benefits to individual households. The town was advertised as a spa and a shopping centre, perhaps in a bid to rival Cheltenham.

The focus at Laurie's new school was primarily on technical skills as opposed to the more academic bias of its neighbour, the Marling Grammar School. The Marling was founded in 1887, largely through the efforts of a local philanthropic family who piously hoped for 'some worthy and permanent provision made for the better education of the middle class and the pick of the working class, who form the backbone of this country'. Equality of opportunity may have been their intention, but the fees – around £9 a term for boys under twelve, £12 a term for the older pupils – put the school beyond the reach of most local families, even though some scholarships were offered. So in 1908 an alternative school opened, at first known as the Stroud and District Craft School. Originally it had just twenty-five boys and no building of its own. Some lessons in textiles were given at the Brimscombe Polytechnic. In response to demand a new free school was built in 1910 at Downfield, financed partly from the local rates.[1]

Some traders at first opposed the building, arguing that it was unnecessary to spend public money on training boys who would afterwards go to work for wealthy mill owners. But educationists approved of the school and regarded it as a model of its kind. In 1921 its name was changed to the Stroud and District Central School for Boys, and applicants were admitted on the basis of a written test and an interview. Boys came from twenty-five local schools, and competition for places was fierce.

In 1926, the year after Laurie joined the school, only thirty-two boys were accepted out of eighty-one candidates. One of the school's benefactors at that time was Jack Margetson, chairman of a local mill and vice-chairman of the school governors. He contributed funds for cricket gear and sports cups, books for the library and equipment for scientific experiments.

For a while Stroud Central School was run in conjunction with what became Stroud Technical College, and in Laurie's time the headmaster, F. P. Fuller, commuted between the two sites on a motor cycle.

Wilfred Robinson, a retired college lecturer, born in Nailsworth in 1914 just a few months after Laurie, was his classmate at the school for four years. 'I think my studies suffered from sitting next to him – he was always up to something. You could say that he distracted me. I wish I'd known he was going to be famous; I'd have kept notes.' He remembered especially the two of them doing woodwork, a compulsory subject at the school and one that Wilfred particularly enjoyed. He remembered Laurie as having been an entertaining classmate.

Music was a significant feature of the school, and this reinforced Laurie's love of the violin. Concerts were given on parents' evenings, and he used to perform at them. Jack Sollars of Stroud, born in 1911, knew the school at the time. He recalled: 'We heard that Mrs Lee turned up on her bicycle one day, dashed it against the wall and charged in to ask the headmaster for an explanation for the way Laurie had been treated in class.' It is possible that the young Laurie was bullied, and the picture of the schoolboy that emerges is of a dreamy lad, rather solitary and indifferent to sport.

Jack Sollars was a friend of Laurie's older brother Jack, who from the Marling School went on to study on a film course at the Regent Street Polytechnic (now Westminster University). Some years later Laurie's brother worked on pioneering British documentaries with the General Post Office Film Unit, later the Crown Film Unit, and this led to a distinguished career in feature film directing.

The seven young Lees and Annie were a close-knit family group in spite of their age range. Jack and Laurie shared many boyhood activities. Tony, a more introverted child, was perhaps the odd one out among the sons. Laurie described Tony telling himself interminable stories and playing solitary games, which suggests that the three brothers were creative in different ways during their teens: Jack the budding film-maker, Laurie the violinist, Tony the story-teller.

Royston and Marjorie Fry of Cainscross, born in Stroud in 1916 and 1919 respectively, met at local dance classes and married in the 1940s. Royston's memories of the Lee family go back to his childhood, when he lived down the road from Emma Lee's sweet and tobacco shop in Wallbridge, long since demolished to make way for a ring road. 'We used to go in there to buy a stick of liquorice or some gob-stoppers for a penny or get the *Citizen* newspaper when it came in the afternoon from Gloucester. We called her Granny Lee. She always kept a sharp eye on us boys and the sweets. I never saw her husband in the shop; I think he had some other job. But the grandsons, Laurie and his brothers, came to visit in the school holidays. I was the same age as Tony, so we played together a bit.'

Later Royston Fry was a contemporary of Tony and Laurie at the Stroud Central School, where he and Laurie learned to play the violin together. 'We had lessons in our lunch-hour with the physical education master, Mr Trevor Pratt. We paid sixpence an hour, about a dozen of us. Laurie was the best player. Afterwards we'd play cricket with the violins as bats and some sticks for stumps, although I don't think Laurie joined in.'

Marjorie Fry worked at the Co-op, as Reg had done, and remembered seeing Annie when she visited relatives in Slad. 'My grandparents knew her. I think they thought she was quite an eccentric lady. Of course some of my family went to Slad Village School, too.' By 1963, a few years after the publication of *Cider with Rosie*, Laurie's fame had spread round the district and he was in demand for public events. Marjorie Fry recalled the centenary of the Cainscross and Ebley Co-op, one of the earliest Co-op centenaries in the country, where the writer was asked to judge a beauty contest and crown the Centenary Queen. He accepted the invitation with enthusiasm.

As schoolboys brothers Jack and Laurie respected each other's talent: Jack the cricketer and rugby player for Stroud Town, Laurie the amateur musician. Jack told me: 'Laurie and I shared a love of books. We were very close as young boys, but in 1926 an event occurred that divided us and we fell out for a while.' He would say no more.

Barbara Tittensor of Charlton Kings (born Barbara Smith in Horsley in 1916) knew the Lee brothers when they were at school in Stroud. She and her friend Phyllis Hawkes attended Stroud High School for Girls. She recalled: 'Phyllis went out with Jack Lee, and a whole set of us from various schools played cricket in a field at Edge and sometimes went swimming. Once we cycled to the Edge Inn and bought our first packet of Woodbines. Later on there were dances at Nailsworth. We had to walk there in our wellies and hide them under a bush when we changed into our dancing shoes. Laurie was a rather thin, shy boy. He didn't stand out, and you couldn't imagine that he would become a celebrity. I don't recall him having any girl-friends then.'

She qualified as a teacher and during the Second World War taught in Woodchester, south of Stroud. 'I joined the Fire Service part-time and while I was fire-watching I met Laurie's cousin, Joan Light. Her father was Annie's brother Charlie, the famous woodsman who had fought in the Boer War. Joan and her married sister Edith and their parents lived in some woodmen's cottages at Horsley. We got quite friendly.' Sometimes Laurie's mother would visit her relatives at Horsley. 'We all called her Auntie Annie. I'd say she was a bit feckless but a very caring and warm-hearted person, just as Laurie described her in his book. Once we all went for tea at Slad. Auntie Annie stayed in her cottage until she had to go into a nursing home at Painswick. I loved *Cider with Rosie*. It was my Cotswold childhood too.'

The Light and Lee cousins went to different schools, in Gloucester and Stroud, but they still met now and then at family gatherings, and cricket was a passion. Charlie Light, brother of Joan and Edith, recalled: 'When I was thirteen or fourteen I saw Jack and Laurie's father, Reg, at a cricket match. He had spectacles and a moustache, and he was quite different from us. We Lights are all eccentric, you know.'

Annie was at Charlie's twenty-first birthday party, and a rather indistinct photograph shows a charismatic figure posing near him, hand on hip, in a dark dress with a high frilled neck. She would have then been fifty-five and was still a good-looking woman. A year later, shortly before he set out on his travels, Laurie spent Christmas with the Lights at Rendcomb. 'He brought his violin – he was a very good player – and the neighbours came round and we had a wonderful time. He was very good company,' said Charlie.

Among Laurie's contemporaries in the 1920s at the Central Boys' School were boys who became councillors, clergy, the chairman of Stroud Magistrates, a mill director and an international footballer. The subjects taught covered a broad spectrum. Music, French and art were on the curriculum. The deputy head, T.V. Pratt, worked at the school for forty-four years; he did much to encourage an interest in music in his students. Laurie wrote little about his later schooldays, but evidently his education did nothing to lessen his love of books. Whatever else school offered or did not offer, it encouraged his compulsive reading.

Years later, in a piece he contributed to the *New York Times Book Review* called 'True Adventures of the Boy Reader', he wrote: 'In those Cotswold villages of the twenties we may have been literate, but we were by no means literary.' In the absence of radio, then a novelty, or regularly delivered newspapers the Bible was, he recalled, a major influence. He and his schoolfellows absorbed an oral tradition of language, and he said that even to that day he was troubled by any form of language that could not easily be spoken aloud.[2]

He read in bookshops on his way home from school and so discovered the classics. A collected set of Dickens's works was rescued by him from a bonfire, and he was 'borne straight away into the stews of old London'. His feeling for narrative must have owed much to the films shown in Stroud cinemas, where for sixpence children could watch silent Westerns, Charlie Chaplin comedies or Gloria Swanson romances.

The *New York Times Book Review* feature included one of Laurie's few references to the years just after he left school: 'My decline was now rapid, and damnation near. It was finally completed at fifteen. I had started work as an office boy in the town, and one day a travelling salesman came in and offered me my own library at a shilling a week. I ordered Lawrence, Shaw and Huxley's *Brave New World*, Gogol, Engels and Marx.'

The job as office boy, which he started at fifteen, was with the Stroud Building Society, where Alan Payne of Rodborough (born in 1912 and eventually to become Chief Executive of the Stroud and Swindon Building Society) knew Laurie well. 'In 1930 Mr Bob Perry, Laurie's master at the Central School, asked my father, Walter Payne, whether he had a vacancy in his office for "a bright boy".' His father, partner in a local firm of chartered accountants, was also secretary of the local building society.

'Laurie as office boy came under the direct control of Teddy White, the Chief Clerk. He was ex-Army Pay Corps and ruled his staff with a rod of iron. He had a violent temper so we juniors were terrified of him.'

Alan Payne remembered the junior staff pay as being no more than ten shillings a week and doubted whether Laurie ever got a rise. 'The office boy was at everyone's beck and call to run errands, including fetching packets of cigarettes for senior staff. His main duties were to make tea for everyone in the afternoon, to be responsible for the postage and to write up the society's ledgers by hand. The office boy was involved in almost everything, so it gave him a good insight into how the office was run. Laurie would cycle to work from Slad, often with his violin slung over his back. When work was slack he would write poems on scraps of paper and leave them around the office. When the office closed for lunch he would play his violin in the room downstairs. This infuriated the senior staff, but he eventually found he could make use of the boiler room without disturbing anyone.'

Alan worked with Laurie for eighteen months from January 1933. 'I realized how unhappy he was, so it was no surprise when my father sent for me in June 1934 and told me: "Lee has resigned. You will take over as office boy immediately." I was shown a note in Laurie's handwriting, which he had left in the stamp drawer, saying: "Dear Mr Payne, I am not suited to office work and resign my job with your firm. Yours sincerely, Laurie Lee." For three years, like Laurie, I was the stooge of everyone in the office.'[3]

In a radio interview Laurie gave his version of how he left the building society: 'I earned seven shillings a week for four years, then they paid me a pound a week. I left a note saying "I think we'd get on better if our ways parted." Next day I walked off to Southampton with a blanket, some treacle biscuits, my violin and two books.'[4]

While he was working as a clerk Laurie continued to live in Slad and commute to Stroud, playing his violin at village concerts and dances, participating in shows put on by the Slad Players, enjoying village cricket and other local events. 'When I was fourteen or fifteen I started a village dance band. We learned the tunes by ear and went to all the villages round, playing for dances and whist drives. Then I joined the Painswick Orpheans. We had trumpet, sax, drums, guitar, piano and me on the fiddle. We were very grand and wore dress shirts on special nights.' It was around this time that he began writing poetry.

In a television film made in his eighties Laurie paid tribute to a friend from his teens, Frank Mansell, descendant of countless generations of a Cotswold family, who grew up on a farm at The Camp village. He was a postal official, a talented fast bowler, an amateur astrologer and friend of Laurie and, like him, a poet. 'Frank was a Cotswold man, as Cotswold as a drystone wall.' They met mainly at the Butchers' Arms in Sheepscombe, where Frank played for the local cricket club and members of Laurie's mother's family still lived. In the pub they read aloud each other's poems. Frank wrote two poems in memory of schoolfellows who had died in the war, and he published a collection called *Cotswold Ballads*. This verse from 'Cotswold Lad' is typical:

> Where fields are girt with Cotswold stone,
> Where Cotswold kind go reaping,
> Among the folk he called his own
> The Cotswold lad is sleeping.[5]

In old age Laurie told a tale of the two of them giving a recital to an audience at Cheltenham Ladies' College: 'Someone said: "Any questions?" "Yes. What makes a true poet?" And Frank said: "Never get married. It's death to poetry."' Frank died in 1979, aged sixty, but Laurie used to visit his grave in Miserden Churchyard and sometimes would recite Frank's poems.

There are hints that Laurie had plenty of brief passions in his late teens, although none to be compared with that first cidrous encounter with the eponymous Rosie. He had girl-friends at the Whiteway Colony near Miserden, a community set up by a group of Londoners who arrived on bicycles in the early years of the century. The aim was to live by Tolstoyan principles, and they bought forty-one acres at £7 an acre, to be shared among a few dozen families who would build their own homes and be self-supporting. Some believed in free love. A century later Whiteway keeps something of its original character, involving collective ownership of the land and committee management.

There were village hops and no doubt a visit or two to the back row of the Picture House or the Empire. Laurie summed up his teenage years in 'First Love', written for *Vogue* magazine: 'I don't think I ever discovered sex; it seemed to be always there – a vague pink streak running back through the landscape as far as I can remember. This was probably due to my English country upbringing, where life was open as a cucumber frame, and sex a constant force, like the national grid, occasionally boosted by thundery weather.'[6]

They were inseparable for him, love and the Gloucestershire land-scape. But the world was changing, he had sea blood in his genes, he felt restricted by village life and the constant pressure to get married. And so at nineteen he left home, fiddle under his arm, to make his way on foot on the open road. London beckoned.

6
The Open Road

I wasn't the first lad to run away to London. They've been doing it for
generations . . . and they do it with the image always in their minds of
returning one day . . . to lay their trophies at the villagers' feet, and
watch the old boys gasp.

– 'An Obstinate Exile'

LAURIE trudged south through Malmesbury, Chippenham and
across Salisbury Plain, enjoying his weekday freedom, making
detours if anything interested him, composing poems in his head. It
has been said that he chose to go to London in this roundabout way
because he had never seen the sea. This is unlikely, for he wrote more
than once of charabanc outings from Slad to Weston-super-Mare. It is
more likely that he picked Southampton as a port known to his grandfather and great-grandfather. Perhaps he felt the call of the sea, as John
Masefield described it in his poem 'Sea Fever', and surely the sea was
in his blood.

Malmesbury and Chippenham were grey-stone towns that he could
compare with Stroud. Then came the great open spaces of Salisbury
Plain. The downland is barer than the landscape of the Cotswolds and
round-topped, lacking secret wooded valleys and studded with prehistoric burial mounds. The Cotswolds have them, too, and Laurie was
aware of Bronze Age barrows and Iron Age hillforts near his home. Yet
in his 1969 autobiography, *As I Walked Out One Midsummer Morning*,
with its account of his long march, he never mentioned these unmiss-
able landscape features.

He spent a week working his way south, camping at night, noting
the giant sweep of a dry terrain that looked to him as if it had been
grazed by mammoths. Salisbury Plain to him seemed vast. If he
followed the most direct route he must have passed within a mile or
two of Stonehenge. Evidently it made no impression (yet he must have

read *Tess of the d'Urbervilles*), or perhaps its pre-tourism isolation caused him to pass it by.

His first major landmark was the spire of Salisbury Cathedral. In Salisbury it was market day, a comfortingly familiar sight. Reading Laurie's autobiography it is easy to forget that this was a twenty-year-old lad, totally unworldly, glad to see reminders of home.

When he reached Southampton he was fascinated by the docks. It was 1934, and the quayside was choked with exotic shops. Laurie mentions tattooists and fortune-tellers, shops selling kites and Chinese paper dragons. Everywhere he heard the unknown languages of sailors from around the world. This was the first of many global ports that would seduce him in his lifetime: Bombay, Beirut, Caribbean harbours, Cádiz, Amsterdam, Galway – he wrote with enthusiasm about them all.

That first week in Southampton Laurie slept in a doss house by the docks for a shilling a night and earned his keep by busking. It was a huge and alarming adventure for a countryman who had never slept away from home before this journey. 'I drew my violin from my coat like a gun . . .' – an image he uses again in his poem 'Music in a Spanish Town' – and to his surprise he was neither arrested nor told to stop playing. The pennies piled up, and he felt this way of making money was almost too easy – but it was a trick he could always earn a living by.

He learned which tunes were most productive and which were most likely to bring out the generosity in people: 'Loch Lomond', 'The Rose of Tralee' and 'Ave Maria' were particularly popular. 'I was out in the streets from morning to night in a gold-dust fever, playing till the tips of my fingers burned.' Having thoroughly milked Southampton he moved on to Gosport, Chichester (where he was chased from outside the cathedral by the police), Bognor Regis (where he camped on the beach in the company of a sixteen-year-old girl) and Littlehampton (where he was moved on again by the police, who advised him to try Worthing). The Gloucestershire innocent was fast becoming a man of the world.

Worthing suggested to him a Cheltenham-on-Sea, peopled by

bejewelled invalids who loved his tunes. He collected thirty-eight shillings in an hour – more, he noted, than a farm labourer earned in a week. This was enough to keep him going on foot to London, joining forces with a great army of jobless travellers 'on the treadmill of the mid-thirties'. This was the Depression, and jobs were hard to find. Laurie's experience as an office clerk, his violin skills and his way with words would be of little advantage in the city.

He stayed first with the family of an American girl-friend whom he had met at the Whiteway Colony. In its early days the Whiteway Colony, only a few miles from Slad, was an idealistic refuge for young would-be writers and families disillusioned with the materialistic society. Laurie was desperately in love, but Cleo wanted only to discuss politics. Her father, disapproving, found him a job as a builder's labourer for £2 5s. a week and a room over a café in Putney. For a year he worked as a wheelbarrow pusher, carting cement up the scaffolding of three ugly blocks of flats. In his free time he explored the City of London, haunted the exotic foreign cafés of Soho, attended concerts and the ballet. All this yielded material which he later mined for articles and *As I Walked Out One Midsummer Morning* – the title is a line from one of the folk songs he played on his violin.

As a window on the 1930s these writings are unique. He saw London as 'a rustic confusion'. Buses rattled, costermongers with their ponies shouted their wares, families set off at weekends on bicycles and tandems. Private cars were few, and Laurie observed that a car parked outside a terraced house might mean 'a doctor or a death'. He saw 'prim little taxis like upright pianos' and horse-drawn drays loaded with beer or flour. He recorded what few Londoners at that time would have thought worth recording: a tot of whisky cost sixpence, half a pint of beer fourpence ha'penny, twenty cigarettes elevenpence. His impressions of London, seen with the poet's eye of a twenty-year-old, can be read in the poem 'Sunken Evening' and the essay 'An Obstinate Exile', broadcast by the BBC.

Later he lived in 'the drawers in the human filing cabinets that stand in blank rows down the streets of Kensington and Notting Hill' – a vivid metaphor for the uniform terraces of west London. He

analysed young men's reasons for migrating from a 'creamy village life
. . . to become chief inspector of inkwells at the Ministry of Boil and
Trouble'. They do it, he speculated, to confound their elders, to show
off, to prove their free will. These were his reasons, along with an as
yet unadmitted ambition to live by writing.

So his disillusion was all the sharper. He felt that he had forgotten
'the tricks and trades of the village' and he saw London as a gross
place, out of focus and out of scale. Yet it was for many young provin-
cials quite simply the greatest show on earth. Remembering the free
field harvest of the Cotswolds, he marvelled that people had to buy
mushrooms and cow parsley. Gloucestershire pigeons had swooped out
of high trees; city pigeons padded after him 'like spivs'. Wet grass at
home smelt of milk and honey; wet pavements smelt of boots and
cigarettes.

His observation was detailed and exact, although committed to
print years later. 'I come from generations of Cotswold farmers. I have
inherited instincts that are tuned to pastoral rhythms . . . London cannot fulfil those instincts, and I for my part cannot lose them.' There
would seem to be inconsistency in his afterwards spending more than
twenty years in a place in which he felt an exile. Yet he would justify it
by arguing that he had to write from a distance about the places that
impressed him.

The poem 'Sunken Evening', precise and witty, reflected an alto-
gether more light-hearted view of a young man's London, seen as an
underwater fantasy world. Prawn-blue pigeons feed, lobster-buses
crawl, a church sinks like a wreck, 'the oyster-poet, drowned but dry',
rolls his pen like a pearl; and night 'trawls its heavy net/And hauls the
clerk to Surbiton'. Laurie could see London as depressing and ensnar-
ing but also an entertaining and amusing place. His own view of the
city may have been similarly ambivalent, two landscapes in one, a
love–hate relationship.

He could go to the cinema for ninepence, a theatre for a shilling. In
his memoirs he mimicked Cockney slang with a sure ear and vividly
re-created his working comradeship with ex-convicts and building site
workers on strike for better conditions. Their leader was a comrade

whom Laurie saw as a prototype of worker-heroes on early Soviet posters. So he joined the Communist Party and 'tasted the first sweet whiff of revolution'.

Suddenly the job ended; the flats were built and he had nowhere to go. It was peacetime, and he figured that he could travel anywhere in the world. France, Italy, Greece meant nothing to him, but he knew one phrase in Spanish – how to ask for a glass of water – so Spain chose itself. He bought a ticket from Southampton to the fishing port of Vigo near the Portuguese border for £4 and dallied during his last days in London with a lovely girl called Nell from south London. In May 1935 Laurie Lee set sail for Spain to begin the most adventurous phase of his life.

7
Spanish Landscapes

In the street I take my stand
with my fiddle like a gun against my shoulder,
and the hot strings under my trigger hand
shooting an old dance at the evening walls.
                    – 'Music in a Spanish Town'

THE story of Laurie's first Spanish journey finally appeared in print in 1969, nearly thirty-five years after the event. *As I Walked Out One Midsummer Morning* is a middle-aged man's account of a twenty-year-old's experience. It also gives a very English view of Spain. Laurie disembarked from the Southampton ferry at the Atlantic port of Vigo at dawn on a July morning. It was his first sight of a foreign city, and it made him think of a rust-corroded wreck.

David and Anna Kenning, a water-colour artist and a writer respectively, followed in Laurie's footsteps sixty years later. They arrived by road in June (the Southampton ferry went out of business when air travel to Spain took over) and unexpectedly met an east wind. The puzzling sight of 'patches of grey felt' turned out to be oyster beds, and they succumbed to the lure of succulent fish meals, whereas Laurie had to start his Spanish travels on bread and dates. Vigo was still barnacled, as when Laurie was there, but traffic had driven out the donkeys and glossy shops replaced the bootblacks.[1]

Vigo today is no longer such a busy shipping centre, although it is Spain's chief fishing port. A few cruise liners call in, and fish container ships are based here. It still has steep cobbled streets, a fish market and shellfish taverns by the harbour – too expensive for a backpacker with a few coins in his pocket. Guidebooks mention Vigo as the starting point for many Galicians emigrating to South America, as offering the first view of southern Europe for incoming Caribbeans and as the place where Laurie Lee's Spanish journey began.

Anxious to be on the road, he bought some bread to go with his knapsack, fiddle, blanket and spare shirt and set out across the country. For a twenty-year-old with no Spanish, just a few pesetas and no very clear idea how he would earn a living, it was a risky venture. This was 1935, long before the days of mass tourism, hitch-hiking or globe-trotting students.

Three things strike the reader of *As I Walked Out One Midsummer Morning*: Laurie's ability to conjure up a scene or a landscape in a single sentence, his constant need to draw visual comparisons between Spain and England and his capacity to make friends. The young Englishman, naïve, unworldly, almost penniless, speaking only his mother tongue, was accepted everywhere. His violin talked for him.

The aim of David and Anna Kenning was to record in paintings and words their impressions of Laurie's route. David Kenning later exhibited his travel paintings, taking in views of Vigo Bay, cornfields in Zamora and Segovia, Cádiz from the sea and red roofs in Málaga. His wife's journal provided text to go with the paintings. Vigo, she said, appealed to them with its oyster beds, its fish dishes and the shining hair of its women ('coils of dripping tar', Laurie had called them). Laurie, however, had given himself no time to sample any of these delights.

As he travelled south he exchanged his memories of the grassy Cotswolds for a landscape at first barren, treeless and windswept. 'Wild and silent, it rolled rhythmically and desolately away.' Galicia has been likened to Ireland with its Celtic culture and Atlantic gales. For his first night in Spain Laurie slept alone on a rocky hillside where wild dogs kept him awake. It must have gone through his mind often that this was a crazy and dangerous adventure.

He struck out south-eastward on a track through the hills – a map does not seem to have figured among his possessions – and plodded towards medieval Zamora in Old Castille, reflecting that his Stroud schooldays had taught him about Spain only that Seville had oranges and Barcelona had nuts. More landscapes unrolled before him, with eagles, gorges, ruined castles, goatherds. Everything seemed to fuse in the violent heat, yet these first Spanish landscapes were vividly remembered when Laurie came to write about his travels thirty years later. Landscapes, wherever he found them, were his muse.

A chance meeting with three Germans playing 'Tales from the Vienna Woods' encouraged the notion that he too might fiddle his way through Spain. He played for his supper for the first time at a farmer's house that he stumbled upon among the wheatfields at harvest time. The family demanded music and he gave them an Irish reel, a fandango he had learned in Zamora and more dances which set them whirling.

In Toro the inhabitants were celebrating their patron saint's day with a candlelit procession led by drum and trumpet, and for the first time Laurie felt alone and far from home: 'Suddenly I found myself wishing for a face I knew, for Stroud on a Saturday night . . .' Next day, the hottest of the year, he foolishly plodded on until he was overcome by sunstroke and hallucinations. The heat seemed to batter the earth and he dreamed of green English fields with cows standing knee-deep in reedy streams – a recurring image in his poems. Eventually in a village bar he was revived, given ice to suck and offered mineral water and ham. The friendly locals were curious and intrigued, discussing his presence animatedly. This was the first Englishman on foot they had encountered. The semi-conscious Laurie was bundled into a car and driven to Valladolid – his first lift in Spain.

In this town officials created a licence allowing Laurie to busk: 'A licence is hereby granted to Don Lorenzo Le [*sic*], that he may walk and offer concerts through the streets of this City.' Gradually he became familiar with variations in the brown waterless landscapes of Central Spain and slept in villages that were like desert oases. Buildings and characters played their part, but it was the landscapes that registered most sharply as he stored up images for future poems and memoirs. He wrote of the 'arrested moment of casual detail, the unsorted rubbish of now'.

He carried on to Segovia, with its mighty Roman aqueduct and storks roosting on chimneys, and then towards Madrid, a city of tram bells, false marble and dilapidation. Here was a cityscape, the first since London, and he reacted as strongly to it as to the Spanish countryside. One café-crawl took him to 'a raffish little lane, half Goya, half Edwardian plush, with café-brothels full of painted mirrors'. Laurie's first experience of Madrid – he was to return in strangely different circumstances – was confined to shady bars and alleys where he played operatic airs and, as always, made friends. One companion was Concha, who found him some new trousers and made the sign of the Cross before climbing into bed with him.

In Toledo, as he played outside a café, he made the acquaintance of the South African poet Roy Campbell and his family, who took him under their wing and became lifelong friends.[2] In Toledo he felt at home and stayed awhile. The Campbell family entertained Laurie handsomely and saw him off on his way to Cádiz. It was three months since he had left Vigo. Now it was September, and he crossed a landscape of purple evenings, thundery dawns and 'herds of black bulls grazing in fields of orange dust'.

The long-expected border of Andalusia was crossed at last after Laurie had ridden on a mule and struggled through the blasts of the sirocco. So he came to Seville and the banks of the Guadalquivir, which would feature later on in his verse and drama, and followed the river to the sea. Outside Seville the Guadalquivir reminded him of the Thames near his London home in Putney, and he commented that in the village of Triana the cockerels strutted like Aztecs. The Guadalquivir was as busy as the canal at Paddington, he wrote, yet it was from here that Columbus had set sail and 'the leaky caravelles of Magellan, one of which was the first to encircle the world'. These words give a clue to the inspiration for his second play, *The Voyage of Magellan*, broadcast in 1947.

Then on to Cádiz. Anna Kenning, in her journal, noted that Cádiz in the 1990s had Russian street musicians playing Strauss, much as Laurie's Germans had played in Zamora. She was intrigued by Laurie's comments on the number of disabled beggars and homeless people in the city on the eve of the Civil War and discovered that Cádiz in 1995 still had a homelessness problem and the highest unemployment figures in Spain. (She also recorded that it had the narrowest streets and tallest houses she had seen anywhere.)

Not remaining long in the city, he moved on eastwards where the coastal plains of Andalusia suggested prairies to him, an Arizona-like landscape, where bulls wandered over the pampas like buffaloes. Eventually he slept overlooking Gibraltar and caught the ferry across to the Rock – 'an interloper, looking as though it had been towed out from Portsmouth'.

Moving east to Málaga he found 'an untidy city on the banks of a dried-up river' rather than the Saracen stronghold his reading had led him to expect. For a while he hung around the city playing his fiddle and spending his nights in an inn courtyard among mules and mountain traders. Soon he gravitated towards the European expatriate community he found 'in their hideouts behind the Cathedral'. Today there is still a cluster of small dark bars and old hotels patronized by expatriates of many countries.

When the rains came Laurie bedded down, for a peseta a night, in a six-bed room at the inn with a circus troupe. Then came disaster: his violin disintegrated and his income dried up. Briefly he earned his keep by acting as guide to British tourists from a cruise ship, until he met a young German who had been abandoned by his girl-friend. He obligingly gave Laurie a violin she had left behind.

With winter coming on Laurie decided to settle in a small fishing port sixty miles from Málaga, with two hotels and some unrealized potential as a tourist centre. This was Almuñécar, now a major Costa del Sol resort. He called it Castillo, after its ruined castle, once a Moorish fortress, and he spent seven months there as a hotel musician and odd-job man. With a German accordionist he performed arias, serenades and dance music for residents in a newly built hotel.

Here was yet another landscape Laurie could not help comparing with familiar British scenes: 'Castillo was . . . grey, almost gloomily Welsh . . . part of the Castle was a cemetery, part of the Town Hall a jail, but past glories were eroding fast.' Almuñécar was first settled by the Phoenicians, who called it Sexi. The Romans too had left their mark: an aqueduct, a salt factory and some tombs. Laurie made many friends in Almuñécar then and on subsequent visits, including the Mayor, and his rapport with the town lasted all his life. His most dramatic memories of the place, and indeed the most unforgettable incidents of *As I Walked Out One Midsummer Morning* took place in the weeks in early 1936 leading up to the outbreak of the Civil War.

It is impossible to say how many British visitors have stayed in Almuñécar looking for signs of Laurie Lee's Castillo. He vividly described its life, its people, its tension, as war drew nearer. A waiter called Manolo looked after him when he was drunk – wine was absurdly cheap – and Laurie rejoiced when a Popular Front alliance government was elected in February 1936. In Castillo landowners on one side and workers on the other drew up their battle lines. Laurie tells that he was persuaded to carry a secret message concerning some hand-grenades to a Republican hill-farmer. He did so willingly; his sympathies were entirely with the left.

By May there was bombing and arson. Even Almuñécar's church, the centre of most people's lives, was damaged. Labels began to be attached to the adversaries: the workers called themselves Communists; the Falangists became Fascists. The Republicans hung out their red flag over the Town Hall.

In mid-July the war reached Málaga. Franco had flown from the Canary Islands and led an invasion with the Moroccan units of the Spanish army. Málaga was one of the first mainland towns to fall. Aircraft and tanks threatened Almuñécar – indeed the port was shelled in error by a destroyer in the bay, which later turned out to be friendly. Bridges were blown up, the casino burnt down.

Only days later Laurie woke to see a British Navy destroyer off the coast, sent from Gibraltar to rescue stranded British nationals. He would have liked to stay but felt he had no choice. An excited crowd, he wrote, rushed to the beach to see him and a fellow Briton leave. It was a dramatic moment: 'The King of England had sent a ship for the hotel fiddler and his friend.'

Laurie's Spanish experience had a number of repercussions. His play *The Voyage of Magellan* partly drew on his time in Seville and Cádiz, and the second part of his autobiography, which by the 1990s had sold a million copies, introduced the area around Málaga to a considerable number of British tourists who might not otherwise have visited the region.

In 1987 came the accolade most writers dream of: serialization on television. The actor John Wild played the young Laurie Lee, and much of the filming was done in and around Almuñécar. Interviewed at the time the television series was broadcast, Laurie told a journalist what he recalled with most pleasure from Spain in 1936: 'What I liked especially was this sense of being passed on from one place to another while the girls, who lived mostly behind bars then, were watched by their menfolk very carefully . . . There was one maid at an inn who nudged me down a passage and, opening her blouse, took out two warmed peaches . . . the girls were so locked up and protected then. The sexual hunger was such that almost everyone was writing poetry. As soon as liberation came in the 1960s, poetry stopped. Once you've got all you want, that's the death of poetry.' [3]

He talked in the same interview about other changes in Spain since his first visit. 'I remember looking down and seeing the red silhouette of Madrid on the horizon like the jagged teeth of a saw that had been rubbed into an animal hide. It was a charming city. Today it is five times the size and has lost that peculiarly civilized quality.' He commented that British visitors to Spain now go for its sunshine, not for its culture, but said he had retraced his route with the BBC film director and found quite a few places unchanged from the 1930s. To another interviewer he admitted that the television film had been fairly true to his book, although 'The young man taking my part is much better looking than I was, and the music is by Julian Bream.' Secretly he loved the whole business of having his book filmed, but he was coy about discussing it.

The 'tumbling little village . . . in the midst of a pebbly delta and fronted by a grey strip of sand' which Laurie discovered in 1935 has not entirely disappeared, although it is not a landscape he would recognize today. El Castillo de San Miguel, the fortified headland defended on and off from Roman times until the seventeenth century, still dominates the town. The castle's claim to fame is that it was here that the Moors were finally chased out of Spain in 1492.

A handsome cream-and-white town hall has replaced the old one where Laurie saw local fishermen hang out the first Republican flags. But up the hill the pink brick Church of the Incarnation is unchanged, containing a life-size image of Christ similar to the one he watched carried in procession through the town. Thus there are visible reminders of pre-war Almuñécar, not all of them swept away by highrise apartments and tourist eateries.

The focus of Laurie's stay between autumn 1935 and July 1936 was a square, newly constructed white building on the beach, the Hotel Mediterráneo, one of only two hotels in what was then a very poor fishing village. It was pulled down in the 1980s to make way for a milelong promenade, and under the promenade, exactly where the hotel stood, cluster a few fashionable beach bars.

On the promenade a whitewashed chimney projects above one of the bars; non-functional, it echoes the shape of a chimney seen in old photographs as standing next to the Hotel Mediterráneo. And on this mock chimney are three ceramic plaques of roses, with the following inscription:

El pueblo de Almuñécar en reconocimiento al gran escritor, LAURIE LEE, que vivió en nuestra cuidad en los años 1935–1936, 1951–1952 y la inmortalizo bajo el seudonimo de 'Castillo' en sus obras *Cuando Partí Una Mañana de Verano* y *Una Rosa Para el Invierno*.

Almuñécar, 21 abril 1988

When Laurie saw a picture of the monument, so conspicuous on the seafront, he is reported to have said: 'H'mm, well, the phallus is significant.' And of course he was delighted to be credited with immortalizing a whole town.

So the people of Almuñécar did not forget the young British musician who lived among them fifty years earlier, and every so often there were reminders of him to jog their memories: the two books published in 1955 and 1969, a BBC television film with many minor parts played by local people and occasional return visits from Laurie over the years. In the 1950s he saw Almuñécar at its most depressed, and in *A Rose for Winter* he painted a sad picture of its decline – before the failed sugar-cane crops gave way to orchards of bananas and mangoes and the glory years of tourism rescued the town.

Thereafter Laurie tended to stay in the adjacent smaller and quieter resort of La Herradura. Here in May 1989 he was interviewed by a local journalist, Juan Manuel de Haro, for the weekly paper *Ideal*. He is a true fan. 'I saw Laurie Lee given the town medal by the Mayor, and there is to be a special literary prize bearing his name. He had lots of energy for a 75-year-old, and he obviously enjoyed his life very much. He told me that Almuñécar was very close to his heart – his second town. His visit in the 1930s was a formative time for him, and he found our town friendly and full of hospitality.'

Juan Manuel de Haro also recalled the time when the BBC2 film of *As I Walked Out One Midsummer Morning* was shown in Almuñécar's House of Culture. 'We all applauded, but a fight broke out between two old men who disagreed about what happened when the war came to Almuñécar.' Several people in the town told me that locals prefer not to talk about the war which so divided their community. Indeed at the end of the 1990s few of them have first-hand memories of pre-war Almuñécar, but I talked to two elderly men who not only remember those days but who knew Laurie then. The local historian, Manuel Mateos, born in 1918 and son of a sugar-factory owner, said: 'I was seventeen at the time, and I used to go almost every day to the Hotel Mediterráneo. I never heard Laurie play the violin, but there was a German called Enrico [Laurie's Jacobo?] who played very well. A Swiss called Teodor Weiss [Herr Brandt in the book] owned the hotel, and people of different nationalities stayed there. When the British destroyer came I think Laurie left with a woman. There were just four of us on the beach, not a crowd shouting. That's pure literary invention.'

Several of Manuel Mateos's recollections were confirmed by Máximo Celorrio Ruiz, born in 1914, whose parents owned a textile shop. 'I think Laurie rented a room over our house, opposite the church. There was an older woman too – she might have been English – and a man with a monocle. Laurie was friendly and polite, and he spoke quite good Spanish, but we didn't see much of him. I think they all went away in the English warship, and four or five cars took other non-Spanish people to Málaga. Then officials sealed up his room. I don't know why.' Others have mentioned the man with the monocle, said to be an English writer, but no one has identified him. Gerald Brenan has been suggested, but there is no evidence that he ever stayed in Almuñécar.

A journal produced by the local Institute of Educational Studies in June 1998 published an analysis of Laurie Lee's references to Almuñécar in the light of local knowledge. The authors' research suggested that Laurie's description of the town's poverty and poor fishing catches was not exaggerated and that what little wealth there was depended on sugar-cane. Local memories confirm some of the incidents Laurie describes in the months before the war, but it is agreed that a grand piano was dragged from the Casino, not the church, and bonfires of church images were held on the beach, not in the town square. It is stated that atrocities were committed by men from another village, not from Almuñécar, and there is disagreement about specific incidents of violence. The sugar factory was not destroyed, but the textile shop was taken over and the former owners were paid twelve pesetas a day to run it.[4]

It would be too much to expect locals now in their eighties to remember accurately the events of 1935–6, least of all to recall in detail a hotel employee who had stayed there for less than a year. It was far more than I had expected to meet two lively and articulate survivors of the town before the Civil War and gain some impression of that era from first-hand witnesses. A teacher from the town wrote in another local journal: 'Without doubt the passage of time acts as a filter for memory and facilitates the introduction of elements which did not exist. The book *As I Walked Out One Midsummer Morning* is well worth reading because it involves the reader and lets him take part in a fascinating journey narrated in a masterly way.'

After his dramatic rescue by destroyer from the first explosions of the Civil War, Laurie went by sea to Marseilles, *en route* for England, and found there a small English-speaking community which included his friend Roy Campbell. And in Martigues, a fishing village on the outskirts of Marseilles, he first met a five-year-old Anglo-French girl who would later become the most important person in his life. According to Laurie, she sat on his lap and told him she would like to marry him. In 1998 she recalled: 'I dare say I thought it would be nice to marry him – this Prince Charming – as you do as a child.'

Martigues was home to a Bohemian community of expatriate writers and artists some of whom, particularly Campbell, indulged in a little bullfighting, some old-fashioned jousting from boats (a sport invented by the Romans) and other nautical activities. The Campbells were joined from time to time by Augustus John, the portrait painter, and his colourful family, by D.B. Wyndham Lewis and assorted members of the London arts fraternity. In later years Laurie liked to tell a Campbell legend of Roy fixing Augustus John's wedding among gypsies in the Camargue – a fiction, but it could easily have been fact as far as the John family was concerned. Others who visited Martigues were the sculptor Jacob Epstein and a family of remarkable sisters named Garman; one of them, Kathleen, was Jacob's lover, another, Helen, the mother of the five-year-old girl.

Laurie lingered awhile in this congenial company. In his book *Two Women* he mentions the visit, describing himself in the summer of 1936 as a crumpled 22-year-old; and other writers have recorded that he was there. But the next year is a gap in the autobiographical record, for he did not return to England until August 1937. For most of that year he was in Martigues, among unconventional people who were to remain lifelong friends, so it was not surprising that, on his return, he found England in the summer a dull place, 'snoozing under old newspapers and knotted handkerchiefs'. Almost at once he felt an urge to return to Spain and a guilt at having turned his back on what many young British men saw as a Cause.

In *As I Walked Out One Midsummer Morning* Laurie identified his age as still twenty-two, but this is impossible. Spanish Civil War records pinpoint his sudden departure from Almuñécar as taking place in July 1936 and his joining the Republican Army in December 1937. The year in Martigues signalled his development from violin-playing wanderer to politically conscious freedom fighter: he felt compelled to go back and fight alongside his radical Spanish friends.

His plans to return were complicated by a romantic attachment. The young woman concerned – anonymous in his book – was rich, 'demandingly beautiful', married with two children and, according to Laurie, 'fanatically jealous'. Her name was Lorna Wishart, and she was one of the extraordinary Garman sisters with whom his life became entangled. Despite her attempts to stop him, he set off for the Pyrenees by train via Perpignan. She pursued him by car. After a week of farewells, hysteria, tears and passionate love-making Laurie detached himself to cross the mountains into Spain on foot. They both believed he was going to his death.

8
Laurie's War

Your breathing is the blast, the bullet,
and the final sky.

Spanish Frontier, 1937
– 'A Moment of War'

THE Spanish Civil War evokes in some an image of eager young men
giving their lives for an ideal. This is a simplification. The socialists,
communists and Marxists who came from around the world to fight
under the Red Flag for a democratic people's Spain died wholly in
vain. The Republican cause splintered and betrayed itself and the war
petered out, resulting in a Fascist dictatorship that was to last forty
years.

But to have been there, to have worn the Republican armband and
red scarf, to have frozen half to death in a terrible Spanish winter, to
have handled a gun in sandbagged pits in the mountains; in spite of
the disillusion and defeat, this was for many young men an ideal in
itself. Laurie was one of them, and his memories of that strange war
are recorded in the third part of his trilogy. It is perhaps the frustration,
the hunger and cold that went with being shuttled around from one
improvised billet to another that come through most strongly, but it is
also a very personal reaction to battle.

The book was published in 1991, dedicated simply 'To the
Defeated'. There are poignant line drawings by Keith Bowen, and the
frontispiece reproduces the 23-year-old Laurie's Communist identity
card showing the narrow, anxious face of a fair-haired young man –
across it a rubber stamp with one word legible: 'Commissar' (a senior
Communist political rank in the army).

The book caused a stir because relatively few accounts had been
written by British survivors of the Civil War, and this was by an eye-

witness. In 1996, sixty years after the start of the war, surviving foreign fighters for the Republic were granted citizenship by the Spanish government. Laurie was one of these, but being eighty-two he was not well enough to travel to Spain for the ceremony. It was enough to have told his story, his version of what happened to him there.

After Laurie's death controversy arose as to how far his memories were accurate. Correspondence erupted in the national press; his widow was put in a difficult position, having to defend Laurie's writing against people who claimed conflicting memories of the war. In brief, some argued that there was no evidence, either documentary or hearsay, that he had actually been in the International Brigades or fought at Teruel; the writer's supporters countered that his name appeared on Communist Party and military documents of the time, that reputable histories of the war quoted his memoirs.

It is helpful to check Laurie's reminiscences against those of other participants in the war. It is quite credible that he struggled across the Pyrenees from Perpignan towards Figueras in midwinter. There are ancient trails through the eastern Pyrenees, once used by shepherds, monks and hunters and now by backpackers and ramblers. Other volunteers reached Spain by this route at about the same time, although most had been recruited by national Communist parties and shuttled via Paris or Marseilles.

Jack Jones, later a Commissar in the British battalion of the International Brigades, travelled on foot from Perpignan to Figueras. He told an interviewer that some said it was the toughest part of the war for them. He fought and was wounded at the Battle of the Ebro in 1938. Much later he went on to become general secretary of the Transport and General Workers' Union, a Companion of Honour and champion of pensioners' rights.

His 1986 autobiography, *Union Man*, certainly does not romanticize his Civil War experiences. They form a single chapter in his distinguished life story. His account of life with the International Brigades set out the bare facts. 'The food was pretty awful. We ate it because we were hungry,' he recorded, adding later that the main meal of the day was often bean stew with mule or old goat. When the elderly Spanish anarchist fighting beside him in the trenches at Lérida was killed, he noted laconically: 'Others around me dragged him away and later buried him in a rough shallow grave.'[1] He wrote unheroically about his own wounding: 'There were many casualties and I became one of them . . . Suddenly my shoulder and right arm went numb . . . As night fell I made my own way, crawling to the bottom of the hill . . . The place was like an abattoir; there was blood and the smell of blood everywhere.' When he was asked later if he had killed anyone in Spain, he said: 'Frankly, I don't know, but it's possible.' In battle, he said, men experienced a numbness; their first instinct was self-protection and then to fire in the general direction of the enemy. This seemed to bear out Laurie's memories.

Badly hurt and invalided home to Liverpool after the Battle of the Ebro, Jack Jones threw himself into organizing an appeal which raised £6,000 to send a food ship to Barcelona. His is one of the most factual and convincing British eye-witness accounts of the Spanish Civil War. When I asked if he had met Laurie, he replied that he had encountered him only briefly in recent years and then in television studios.[2]

Laurie, in *A Moment of War*, acknowledged that his means of getting to Spain was bizarre, especially given the weather, when he could have joined groups crossing the frontier by train and lorry if he had known better. His subsequent arrests, interrogations and imprisonments are hard to verify, but his account of Republican internal suspicions, food shortages and appalling weather conditions is borne out by others. Laurie mentioned hunks of dry bread and thin watery soup, sometimes with beans, as a staple diet, supplemented by brandy and wine. Walter Gregory, who travelled from Nottingham to Figueras at almost exactly the same time, and George Orwell, who was already in Spain, told the same story of intense cold and privation.[3] Orwell, in *Homage to Catalonia*, listed the priorities for Republican fighters as firewood, food, tobacco and candles, in that order. Both he and Laurie stressed again and again the bitter cold they endured.[4]

Doubts have crept in over the repeated arrests of Laurie as a spy. On the first occasion he told of being questioned by a Captain Perez who accused him of having landed from a German submarine to spy behind the Republican lines. More convincing was the second of his reported arrests, when he was singled out by an American officer in the Brigades called Sam. This arose because his passport showed that he had been in Spanish Morocco earlier in 1936 when Franco was drilling his army for the mainland invasion. Laurie's excuse, that he had spent a day or two in Morocco on an excursion from Almuñécar, did not impress the loyalists, but they let him go. His interrogator was possibly Sam Wild, later in charge of English-speaking units in the International Brigades.

Laurie's 1937 memories of Albacete, the base camp of the 15th Brigade, included a reunion with Fred Copeman, his Communist mentor and the strike leader on the building site in London on which Laurie had worked two years earlier. This man perhaps corresponds with the Fred Copeman mentioned by Walter Gregory and also with a volunteer of the same name quoted in Hugh Thomas's *The Spanish Civil War* – although he was described here as commander of the British at the Battle of Brunete, an ex-Navy man who did not join the Communist Party until later.[5]

Laurie retold eye-witness accounts by others of the battles of Guadalajara, Jarama, Brunete and Belchite – all of them leading to many British casualties. These tally with accounts in other books, both historical and autobiographical. He referred to numerous other volunteers, including a White Russian called Sasha, but such individuals are identified only by first names.

Tarazone de la Mancha was the training centre for the Brigades, where Laurie had as his commander a Frenchman named Kassell, mentioned also by George Orwell. Here he heard Harry Pollitt, leader of the British Communist Party, give a pep talk and was reunited with Eulalia, an old flame from Figueras. Critics have suggested that the character of Eulalia was borrowed from another author. Tortured by 'almost wolf-like hunger' he and two others scraped together a thousand pesetas for three scrawny farm chickens – to them a banquet after subsisting on boiled swede and donkey bones. No one has queried the details of this particular account, and several of the men named can be traced in other Civil War literature.

Nor do critics question his spell as a propaganda broadcaster with Radio Madrid, reading manifestos, reciting poems and discussing European politics for a distant US audience. It is interesting to note that few of the recent British histories emphasize the role of Republican Radio Madrid. But this can be checked, even the fact that Laurie sought out old friends from pre-war days in the vicinity of the inn where he had stayed on his first journey across Spain. He described being reunited with Concha, one of his earliest Spanish loves.

The most damaging criticisms of Laurie's memoirs refer to the Battle of Teruel. This was a major battle fought between December 1937 and February 1938, a counter-offensive by the Republicans in an attempt to relieve Nationalist pressure on Madrid. Laurie wrote of a four-day blizzard, when men literally froze to death. He and a Portuguese youth were sent up to the Teruel front in a truck with a Russian driver, along a road littered with abandoned vehicles. Snow fell in 'large flaky gusts'. When they bedded down for the night in a barn his coat crackled with frost and his nose stung as if split by skewers. Next morning the bombardment began 'with a clapping of giant hands'. Franco's troops were retaking Teruel. On what Laurie called 'the frozen terraces of Teruel' he recounted how he saw men in rags, men frozen to death, men eating out of buckets like animals. Out of touch with his fellow countrymen, Laurie joined a group of no-hope Spaniards led by an ex-schoolmaster. They gave him an old rifle with the advice that at least he could shoot himself. Next day their position was attacked by Nationalist tanks and Italian aircraft. Their machine gun was put out of action and Laurie became aware of the enemy on top of them – 'boys' and 'Moors'.

The passage that follows is one of the most quoted in Laurie's writings: 'the sudden bungled confrontation, the breathless hand-to-hand, the awkward pushing, jabbing, grunting, death a moment's weakness or a slip of the foot away'. A few lines later he recorded that he had killed a man with shocked, angry eyes. He retreated to the barn and lay as if paralysed and speechless. He recalled hallucinations and 'breaks in the brain' (perhaps warnings of epilepsy). Was this what he had come to Spain for, 'to smudge out the life of an unknown young man in a blur of panic'? The passage seems to ring true and certainly reflected Laurie's non-aggressive personality, yet it has been doubted by Civil War veterans.

The Battle of Teruel is well documented in a number of histories, notably Hugh Thomas's *The Spanish Civil War,* in Walter Gregory's autobiography and in *Voices from the Spanish Civil War*, the recollections of Scottish volunteers who fought in Spain. Nowhere in any of these books does Laurie's name appear. But then why should it?

More problematic is the testimony of Bill Alexander, commanding officer of the British troops at Teruel, so badly injured there that after the battle he was sent home (his replacement was Sam Wild). In 1998, aged eighty-seven, as secretary of the International Brigades Association he insisted in national newspapers and in a radio interview that Laurie had not been present at the Battle of Teruel; as commanding officer he would have at least heard his name, he maintained.[6]

Bill Alexander said that he had been prompted to set the record straight as a new *Oxford History of the Spanish Civil War* had just been published, which quoted from *A Moment of War*. 'I would rather he had called his book a novel rather than autobiography. It didn't happen as he told it.' One who concurred was Simon Courtauld, author of *Spanish Hours.* In an article in the *Spectator* he revealed that Bill Rust, former editor of the *Daily Worker*, had spent time with Laurie in Catalonia and recalled that he failed his medical examination because of epilepsy. According to Bill Rust, Laurie was sent home from Barcelona before the battle. Simon Courtauld said that he asked Laurie in 1995 to talk to him about Teruel but 'he said the memories were too painful'. This is surprising but perhaps credible in view of Laurie's expressed horror of events, but he took it as evidence that some of the writer's memories were invented.[7]

Simon Courtauld also queried Laurie's dates. But his own dating is open to question. He accepted Laurie's statement on the first page of *A Moment of War* that he crossed the Pyrenees in December 1937, and all his arguments stemmed from that assumption. However, a few calculations suggest that it may have been earlier. *As I Walked Out One Midsummer Morning* indicated that Laurie spent a short while in

England, between August and November 1937, before his return to wartime Spain. It is hard to believe that the movements and activities he then described could have taken place in a few short weeks between late December and the main stages of the Battle of Teruel, which was over by February 1938. Christmas was referred to repeatedly, yet more than two weeks must have elapsed since his arrival in Spain. There seems to have been some telescoping of events to emphasize the horrors of winter – the snowbound and freezing landscape underpinned all his reporting.

Simon Courtauld also challenged Laurie's account of the militia practice of basing decisions on voting. He claimed that this had been given up by 1937. But Laurie seems to have been referring to earlier events, perhaps based on hearsay, and surely it is understandable if his memory let him down after more than fifty years.

The uncertainty over dates does not prove that Laurie was *not* present at the Battle of Teruel. Others came to the writer's defence when the controversy erupted in the press. Vernon Scannell, the Yorkshire poet born eight years after Laurie, was one of those who defended *A Moment of War*. Given the nature of the three volumes of memoir, written so many years after the actual events, he asked: 'Does it really matter whether his experiences as a young volunteer in Spain, described so dramatically, are factually true or not?' Vernon Scannell (who himself fought throughout the Second World War) speculated that Laurie, like others of his generation who did not fight between 1939 and 1945, possibly felt deprived – 'so the imagined drama of bloodshed, heroism and sacrifice possessed a powerful fascination for them'.

Barry McLoughlin, an Irishman researching Communist Party history in Moscow, wrote in the *Guardian* that he believed he had evidence of Laurie's involvement in the International Brigades at Teruel: 'Bob Doyle, a Dublin-born Communist, wrote of how he had been put in charge of a group of English-speaking volunteers from Paris to Figueras . . . he singled out "Lawrence Lee" for positive comment. Lee had suffered from fits. His conduct, however, was "excellent" and he showed "willingness to comply with regulations".' Laurie indeed had epilepsy, and this may explain his not being recruited to the Armed Forces in 1939.[8]

Barry McLoughlin cited a similar report on the author made by an American officer transferring with volunteers from Figueras to Albacete. Two minor difficulties remain: Laurie does not ever mention travelling from Paris to Figueras with other volunteers, and his name is misspelled. Barry McLoughlin questioned some details in *A Moment of War*: 'Lee's report that he [was twice arrested as a spy but] emerged more or less unscathed, does not convince me . . . I also have my doubts about the romantic interest . . . English-speaking volunteers tended to say that Spanish women were not very approachable and certainly not sexually available.' Overall, however, he supports the view that Laurie served in the International Brigades.[9]

The debate over whether Laurie officially joined the Brigades is answered in part by his wife Kathy, who told reporters in 1998: 'I have re-read the chapter and it clearly says he was on the edge of the Battle of Teruel with a rag-tag group of people and doesn't claim to have fought with the International Brigades.' Barry McLoughlin's reply to this was that Laurie must be presumed to have joined up if he took part in rudimentary Brigades training in Figueras and Albacete; it was not unusual for volunteers to be found unsuitable and sent home.

The controversy is unlikely to be resolved. Laurie was recalling events fifty years after they had happened. He revisited the area once to retrace his steps, but, as he told Edward Blishen during an interview in 1994, he found little to remind him of 1937. He described lining up at Figueras Station with a motley crew of raw recruits for basic drill before they entrained for the base at Albacete, cheered on by a local band with flowers. He remembered rather vaguely front-line incidents and the constant search for food and tobacco – but he had little to add to the book; hardly surprising after what was now an interval of fifty-seven years.

Some people have questioned whether he was old enough to have joined the International Brigades, but Paul Hogarth, the distinguished illustrator and another Civil War survivor, recalled in a BBC Radio 4 interview in 1998 that recruits were expected to be at least twenty-one years old and without dependants, since the Republicans could not provide pensions. On these counts Laurie would have been eligible.

Reviewing the 1998 controversy, one is bound to ask whether poetic licence led Laurie to embroider his experiences in Spain. It would be surprising if it did not, given his previous writing and the distance of time involved. The only other professional British author who wrote a full-length book as one involved in the war, George Orwell, spells out in factual detail a picture so realistic that one is compelled to believe it. His account, concentrating on the POUM, the party of anti-Stalinist Communists that he supported, is far longer and it was published in 1938, before the war had ended. Here are two complementary pro-Republican accounts to be read side by side, the story of George Orwell the reporter-essayist and Laurie's poet's-eye view.

Further evidence of Laurie's emotional reaction to violence in Spain is expressed in poetry. The poem 'A Moment of War', datelined 'Spanish Frontier, 1937' and therefore contemporary with Teruel, conveyed the author's revulsion:

> The hands melt with weakness
> into the gun's hot iron . . .
> the bowels struggle like a nest of rats . . .
> . . . darkness opens like a knife for you.

The poem also carried a powerful image of blood and of Republican soldiers in typical Communist gear, a simile of night as a red rag over the eyes.

When the literary merit of A *Moment of War* is evaluated, readers will weigh up its emotional impact against what some see as niggling complaints about its veracity. Whether he killed a man or not, whether he was sent home after or before the battle, readers may judge his poetry and prose as inspired.

Under bombardment, the body takes over the mind; it stiffens and melts, the mouth floods and dries, and all one's senses rush to the back of one's neck . . . when a shell hit the ground and exploded nearby the

snow rose in the air like a dirty ghost, and hung there spikily billowing
. . . the landscape around showed all the rubbish of failure, the end of
charity and hope . . . Three soldiers lay propped against a wall, their
bodies half-stripped by the wind. Most certainly they had frozen to
death.

It is hard to believe the poem and the last chapter of the book were
written by someone who was not at Teruel.

9
Wartime London

> We must ignore the budding sun and seek
> to camouflage compassion and ourselves
> against the wretched icicles of war.
>
> – 'The Armoured Valley'

LAURIE returned from the battlefields of Old Castille to a London in the shadow of the September 1938 Munich Agreement. He returned to his old haunts and set about finding a job that would satisfy his growing urge to earn his living as a writer. What may have triggered this ambition was the London arts set within which he moved – survivors of the 1936 Martigues community – and the fact that he was now taking himself seriously as a poet.

The glamorous girl-friend who had sent him money and welcomed him back from Spain at London's Victoria Station was evidently no substitute for a steady income. This he was to find in what had formerly been the General Post Office Film Unit, where his brother Jack worked as a director after finishing his film studies. The unit had been set up initially to publicize various branches of the Royal Mail. Typical pre-war productions were *Man in Danger*, which alerted factory workers to industrial hazards, and *Love on the Wing*, a romantic view of the Post Office airmail service.

On 14 March 1939, roughly a year after Laurie's return from Spain, an event took place which is nowhere mentioned in his published writings. His daughter Jasmine was born.

Jasmine Margaret was the daughter of Lorna Wishart, one of the beautiful Garman women who cropped up from time to time in Laurie's life. She can be recognized as the 'Chanel-scented lover' with whom he spent time before and after the Civil War. In both *As I Walked Out One Midsummer Morning* and *A Moment of War* he wrote lyrically of their passionate affair, identifying her only as married, with two children and living in Hampstead. 'I remember the flowers on the piano, the white sheets on her bed, her deep mouth, and love without honour.' Lorna Wishart, née Garman, was the wife of a publisher and mother of two. Close in age to Laurie, she was closely connected with the Martigues community.

Jasmine's birth certificate names her as the daughter of Lorna Cecilia and Ernest Edward Wishart, publisher, of Acacia Road, St John's Wood, London. She grew up as a Wishart, became an artist and married a Devon cider-apple farmer. Now Mrs Yasmin David, she is the mother of two daughters and a son. When he died, Laurie had three adult grandchildren but none linked to him by name.

Has Yasmin inherited any of her father's interests and talents? She told me: 'I don't play a musical instrument, but I've always loved music – especially Beethoven, Schubert, Chopin and Debussy.' Schubert was held to be Laurie's favourite composer. Yasmin had no special ties with the Cotswolds – the landscapes most familiar to her are Sicily, South Africa and the south-west of England. I asked which of Laurie's works she liked best and she replied: 'I've read all his books, but he was primarily a poet'; this is, of course, how her father would wish to be remembered. She first met her father when she was 'very tiny', but clearly she has always been discreet about their blood-tie. She was present at Laurie's funeral; her name appeared among the mourners but not as a family member. She found the service moving and thought the site of the grave appropriate.

On the eve of the Second World War the General Post Office Film Unit became absorbed into the Crown Film Unit, an offshoot of the newly formed Ministry of Information, where Laurie's brother Jack was a leading light. He said: 'I suppose my brother came to the Crown Film Unit because I was already there. Films I worked on during 1938, 1939 and 1940 were *London Can Take It*, *Merchant Seamen*, *Ordinary People* and *Coastal Command*. Laurie also wrote scenes for my submarine film *Close Quarters*.'[1]

A telegram has survived that Jack and Laurie sent from London on the day war broke out, 3 September 1939. Jack said that at the time they were sharing digs in Putney 'for a short while before Laurie moved away, having other fish to fry'. The wire was addressed to Mrs Lee, Slad, Stroud, and the time of dispatch recorded as 11.35 a.m. – just half an hour after the radio announced the outbreak of war, following Germany's refusal to withdraw its troops from Poland. The message read: 'Don't worry about us – were alright [*sic*] – Jack and Laurie.' In fact Laurie kept in touch with his mother at Slad throughout the war. Annie wrote to him regularly and he visited from time to time. It has been suggested that *Cider with Rosie,* perhaps already germinating in his mind, was based on her memories as much as his.

Early in 1939 the Crown Film Unit produced a film which must have brought back images of the Spanish Civil War for Laurie: *The Warning.* This was advice for communities coping with air raids. There cannot have been many London civilians at the time with more relevant experience than Laurie. The film included footage of Sir John Anderson, head of Air Raid Precautions planning, who gave his name to Anderson shelters: the reinforced garden dugouts erected for families to escape from bomb blast. It was uphill work for a film to popularize these flimsy shelters in advance of the Blitz, but once bombs began to rain down on London the need for such shelters became more and more urgent. People reacted instinctively to air-raid warnings, the eerie fluctuating wail of sirens so familiar to Laurie from Spain.

Since the Lee brothers were never conscripted it seems that their propaganda work was regarded as a reserved occupation, although in Laurie's case his medical history may have exempted him. In a radio interview much later he offered a different explanation: 'I think I was listed in somebody's little book. I went into documentary scriptwriting for films about the Army, the Navy, the North Atlantic convoys, "Dig for Victory" and that sort of thing. And I produced books for the Ministry of Information.' Jack and Laurie were wartime civil servants.

London during the war was not an easy place to live and work: dodging the air raids, making sure one's windows showed no chink of light, sleeping in makeshift shelters or in underground railway stations which at night became huge dormitories where people bedded down with mattresses and flasks of tea. There were of course no street lights.

Torches had to be masked with brown paper, and cigarette smoking in the streets was forbidden.

Laurie moved from one set of digs to another, none too far from the Ministry of Information's sandbagged offices. His pay as a civil servant was not high – around £8 a week – and he lived frugally. Food rationing was tight, with coupons for minuscule amounts of meat, butter, bacon and sugar, so not much needed to be spent on eating. Government canteens, called British Restaurants, sprang up which provided basic meals for workers – meat and two veg, pudding and custard – for two shillings and sixpence. It was best not to try to identify the meat, which was usually grey and gristly.

Buses ran fairly normally – making detours where necessary to avoid overnight bomb damage – and trains ran unless a rail track had been destroyed. As the air raids intensified more and more volunteers were needed to work as air raid wardens, fire-fighters and fire-watchers. One can picture Laurie on a Ministry roof at the height of the Blitz. Between September 1940 and May 1941 London was bombed almost continuously, and by September 1942 more civilians had been killed than servicemen. In inner London only one house in ten escaped damage. The moat of the Tower of London was turned into vegetable allotments, and concerts were held in roofless bombed churches.

In spite of all this, much wartime filming by the Crown Film Unit was done at Pinewood Studios in Buckinghamshire, only half an hour by train from central London and the location for some famous pre-war epics, among them *The Private Life of Henry VIII* and *The Four Feathers*.

Another employee with the unit was John Mortimer, just down from Oxford and not yet famous as Queen's Counsel, playwright and novelist. He gave a hilarious account of life at Pinewood in his autobiography, *Clinging to the Wreckage*, and in his first novel, *Charade*. He was a fourth assistant director, paid £2 a week, helping to produce propaganda documentaries which he regarded as prestigious and boring in equal measure. Much of the time he played cards in a disused prop room among the thrones and four-poster beds of Alexander Korda's pre-war film empire. When he was not travelling to Liverpool on location (he gave the impression it was always Liverpool) John Mortimer spent his nights singing 'Roll Out the Barrel' in local hostelries or fire-watching on the Pinewood Studios roof. 'From time to time a sweet melancholy music could be heard in the corridors . . . it was the poet, Laurie Lee, playing on his recorder.'[2]

So Laurie was beginning to be thought of as a poet, and he had by now learned to play another musical instrument. He was officially a unit scriptwriter, but John Mortimer recalled him continually piping 'like a small sly Pan', appearing more interested in the Spanish war than in the conflict closer to home and highly ingenious in putting off tasks that had to be undertaken. According to John Mortimer, his poetic prose style created difficulties in the documentary film world and it was guessed that his heart was still in Spain serenading pale Spanish beauties.

Shortly after, Laurie resigned from the film unit to work in the publications division of the Ministry of Information, and John Mortimer took his place. He was offered a permanent appointment if he wrote a script for Laurie to approve. He was to write about Watford Junction Station, an unglamorous stop on the main line from Euston. John Mortimer cycled the twelve miles there in his eagerness to get the job, wrote a romantic storyline about a station-master's wife and an American soldier and a month later was appointed official scriptwriter at a salary of £11 a week – 'an almost unthinkable height'. As he pointed out, he had Laurie to thank for the only time in his life when he earned his living entirely as a writer. Soon after he went back to studying for the Bar.

John Mortimer paid affectionate tribute to Laurie at the memorial service half a century later. Their friendship had endured, although it would have been hard to find two men less alike, even in their writing. John Mortimer was nine years younger, Harrow and Oxford educated, a lawyer almost by heredity. He recalled that at Pinewood he and Laurie shared an interest in a beautiful woman called Mavis who drank with them at the Crooked Billet. He described Laurie's works as immortal, making generations of readers happier and wiser, and Laurie himself as funny, ironic and kind-hearted.

Cecil Day-Lewis, later Poet Laureate, was Laurie's closest friend at the Ministry of Information, and for a time Laurie shared a flat off Walton Street, in Kensington, with Cecil and his lover Rosamond Lehmann.

Much of the Ministry's wartime work was undertaken in temporary headquarters in Russell Square, near the British Museum. Here the two poets worked in the Publications Division, under Sir Robert Fraser (later director of the Central Office of Information), editing material produced by various government departments. They helped to edit the official histories of the Battle of Britain, Bomber Command and the Burma Campaign. They had fun, too. Laurie, described by a contemporary colleague as 'volatile' and 'an inveterate joker', was involved in the creation of a spoof periodical called *A Hope for Poultry* (a parody of *A Hope for Poetry*).

During the period of the so-called buzz-bomb raids, when the Germans launched their V-1 rocket attacks on London, Laurie and his colleagues reportedly stayed at their desks even through flying glass and falling plaster. Sean Day-Lewis, Cecil's older son, recalled hearing that Laurie (perhaps finding excuses not to work) acted as an unofficial buzz-bomb spotter, perched on a window ledge with binoculars and a police whistle.

In April 1943 Laurie spent a long weekend with the Day-Lewis family at their home near Axminster in Devon while researching a history of wartime agriculture. At first glance the lifelong friendship seems surprising: there was a ten-year age gap and the two men superficially had little in common. Cecil's father had been a clergyman and his grandfathers middle-class professionals. Cecil went to public school and Oxford, then taught classics at preparatory and public schools. He gave up teaching to become a full-time writer in 1935 – the year that Laurie was setting off on his first Spanish journey.

Cecil was called up for one day only at the start of the war. So he and Laurie came together as editors in a newly created government department producing official war histories. By this time Cecil had written six detective novels under the pseudonym Nicholas Blake and published seven books of verse. Laurie had not yet had any works of literature published. What they had in common were strong left-wing sympathies (they had both been members of the Communist Party), a love of rural England (in Cecil's case Dorset and Devon) and an ambition to live by writing poetry. And each admired the other's work. Laurie was grateful to be taken under the wing of an already established poet, and Cecil wrote to Laurie years later: 'I write too much and you write too little.'

Sean recorded in his 1980 biography of his father that Cecil and Laurie liked and admired each other, 'although they were as different as two complicated men can be. To Cecil it was as if one of his domino opponents at the Red Lion turned out to be a first-rate poet, and not just a poet but a man with a lovely gift of being rooted in his own countryside even when he was somewhere else.' He remembered that Laurie enjoyed Mary Day-Lewis's cooking and sometimes played cricket with Sean and his brother Nicholas. 'But his great skill was making bows and arrows and showing me and my brother how to use them. I think he liked to think he was a boy too, although he was nearly twenty years older than me. Sometimes he had periods of depression, but mostly he was very good company.'³ At this time Laurie was Cecil's closest friend, and Sean hazarded a guess that Cecil would have particularly enjoyed Laurie's sense of 'sly, child-like fun'.

Sean's mother recorded in her diary the time when Laurie dropped everything in mid-1947 and rushed down to Axminster when Cecil was deeply depressed, trying to combine family life with his love for the writer Rosamond Lehmann. The poets stayed closeted in Cecil's study all day, although Laurie had acute toothache; next day he went to a dentist in Seaton to have an abscess treated, while Cecil mowed the lawn. The family were led to believe that it was Cecil comforting Laurie, not the reverse. Mary wrote: 'Cecil and Laurie seem happy . . . and they've decided to go on holiday together. I wish *we* were going on holiday.' So the two men set off for two weeks in Copenhagen. The visit, planned by Laurie to provide 'lots of food, friends and sunshine on the beach', seems to have cured Cecil's depression. Two years later he dedicated to Laurie his *Poems 1943–1947*, several of which refer to the wartime and post-war years in Devon.

Also in the 1940s Laurie stayed with Rosamond Lehmann and her children in their cottage on the Berkshire Downs. In her book *Rosamond Lehmann's Album* she included a photograph of the young Laurie with a guitar, captioned: 'Laurie Lee, who stayed with us for some months in my cottage in 1942 and was doted on by all, including Mrs Wickens, our housekeeper, who fortified him daily with her rice puddings.'[4]

Early in 1950 Cecil and Laurie found themselves together contributing to a BBC radio Third Programme poetry discussion with the poets Patric Dickinson and Henry Reed and the critic Paul Dehn. Cecil wrote that the broadcast went off better than any of them expected, largely because the BBC supplied a number of bottles of wine.

Sean has one other memory of Laurie, at a dinner party during the 1950s given by Cecil and his second wife Jill. 'Afterwards Laurie told me he knew a way of making telephone-box calls without paying for them. I'm not sure if he really thought he could. He fiddled about with some pennies, but of course it didn't work.' In the 1970s Sean wrote to Laurie when he was undertaking research for his biography of his late father. Laurie wrote back: 'He was the man I liked most among my friends and was the kindest to me.'

Within a few months of the outbreak of war Laurie began to get his poems published. As early as April and May 1940 – at the time of Dunkirk – 'A Moment of War' and 'Words Asleep' had appeared in *Horizon*. One looked back to the horror of fighting in Spain, the other to the paradox of death and cockcrow at dawn in Andalusia. Two months later 'Poem', later retitled 'Invasion Summer', reflected the mood of the country after Dunkirk and before the Battle of Britain, when invasion seemed a very real possibility. The poem evoked a sense of unreality – lovers in a hayfield, oblivious of imminent death.

In December 1943, when Laurie was working at the Ministry, *Horizon* published 'Equinox', his vivid hymn to autumn, and two years later 'Field of Autumn', again depicting the destructiveness of the season. His final two poems in *Horizon* appeared in August 1946, a little before a film expedition to Cyprus. 'April Rise' recalled a spring world of happiness but lost innocence and 'Day of These Days' a blissful spring day.

It has been suggested that *Horizon* published Laurie Lee more than any other poet in the 1940s and that most of his early poems appeared first in that magazine. There is not much doubt that *Horizon* was his gateway to success and that the contacts he made through it found him a small niche in the literary establishment.[5]

If he had been asked who most influenced his launch as a poet, Laurie would have said Cyril Connolly. He founded *Horizon*, in its day the most prestigious of literary magazines, and gave a platform to many new young writers in the 1940s. Laurie maintained that it was a girlfriend who showed his work to Cyril Connolly. At any rate, several of Laurie's poems first appeared in *Horizon* in the middle of the decade. He also acknowledged the *Listener* (the BBC magazine which carried transcripts of many radio broadcasts), *Tribune* and *Poets of Tomorrow* as early outlets for his writings. His first solo collection, *The Sun My Monument*, came out in 1944.

Partly through his friendship with Cecil Day-Lewis Laurie now began to take up a position on the fringe of the literary world. An early publisher of his poems was John Lehmann, Rosamond's brother, founder of the *Penguin New Writing* series. It was in this monthly magazine series that 'Thistle' first appeared in July 1946:

> . . . a savage shock of joy
> that set the bees on fire
> and the loud larks singing.

Later it was selected for inclusion in an anthology drawn from ten years of *Penguin New Writing*.

Another fellow-poet and travel writer was Alan Ross, who took over John Lehmann's *London Magazine* and has edited it with distinction for more than thirty years. He shared Laurie's love of cricket, working for many years as a Sunday newspaper sports correspondent.[6] He recalled them watching a game together. 'I remember the local cricket ground where I went to watch a match with Laurie. It was almost vertical.' He thought it unlikely that Laurie had played there. This was certainly Sheepscombe. He also remarked on Laurie's notorious reputation as a joker. 'He used to annoy everybody at parties given at John Lehmann's house at Egerton Crescent in Chelsea by bringing along clockwork toys and running them about on the floor.'

With all his experience of publishing young poets Alan Ross is a well-respected literary critic and he still rates Laurie highly: 'He was a very good poet, very lyrical, who would certainly be published if he were writing today. I'd certainly include his work in the *London Magazine*. His poems exist as vividly as they ever did. He just gave up suddenly, perhaps because when he started writing prose it took all his energies.'

All through the war years, and his work as a civil servant charged with dispensing government information, Laurie never lost sight of the Cotswold valley which provided a vision and a structure for much of his writing. Apart from the poems set in war-torn Spain and wartime southern England, he wrote of violent love, death and passions in the Cotswold landscape which he always carried in his mind.

In 'Poem' (later retitled 'Invasion Summer') he called on the 'unsecretive cuckoo' and 'butterflies in their disorder' to mourn a shot soldier. The whole of the poem 'Juniper' was an erotic fantasy relating the sexual act to the smell of apples, 'cavaliering cocks' and 'bloody leaves of the virginia'. Some poems were purely evocative of a rural world far removed from war and violence. 'The Three Winds' called up the moods and sounds of the seasons; 'The Wild Trees' was the desolate song of an exile longing for the 'fertile wilderness' of his home and his lover.

The closest identification of love and landscape came in 'Song in Midsummer': 'stems of rain grew from the hills/opening blue petals in your throat'. But the poem Laurie will probably best be remembered for from the collection *The Sun My Monument* was 'Milkmaid', which was later selected for an anthology of English love poems, with its hypnotic images of cows having summer mirrored in their eyes, the milking girl's hand distilling the harvest of their day – a cloudy cream – while she, too, dreamed of milk and children.

Although *The Sun My Monument* came out in 1944 – the title of the collection was drawn from a poem celebrating the autumn equinox – his most creative period as a poet came in the ten years following the war. He was in his thirties, with a decade of experience to draw on and freed from the restraints of a demanding wartime job. As he said later about his prose writing, he always needed to be removed in space and time from his subject.

Of the twenty-five poems in that first collection, six reflected the horrors of war, two arose from his pre-war travels and the rest could loosely be considered love poems and verses about landscapes and seasons. The love poems in the collection were erotic and sensual, the war poems full of vivid, physical imagery. No poem was longer than thirty-six lines, and rhyme and fixed metre were rare. The emotional world of the poems was as enclosed as the Slad Valley.

The collection was published by the Hogarth Press in a series called 'Phoenix Living Poets', with the commendation 'A young poet . . . whose brilliant, sensuous and novel imagery won him an enviable reputation'. A later critic wrote: 'We see familiar things more joyously, more seriously, or simply with a greater and unfamiliar depth.' This first book was dedicated 'To Lorna' – Lorna Wishart, his lover before and after the Spanish Civil War, the mother of his now five-year-old daughter.

What makes these early poems unforgettable is their imagery. The butterflies in their disorder represented England waiting for attack; the cocks which 'carve sharp gold scars in the morning' symbolized pre-war Andalusia: the moon climbing 'the beanstalk of the night' was seen over Cyprus; in 'The Armoured Valley' the poet sought 'to camouflage compassion' against the icicles of war; 'Song in August, 1940' featured death sliding down on a string to rape the horizon; in 'The Three Winds' the mood of August sent 'its brick-red breath over the baking wheat and blistered poppy'.

There are echoes in later writing of the verse images: in *As I Walked Out One Midsummer Morning* Laurie described his fiddle as a gun, as he did in 'Music in a Spanish Town'. 'Village of Winter Carols' foreshadowed incidents in *Cider with Rosie,* and one verse looks ahead to a boy's perception of Cotswold winter in an interview given in old age:

> You were adventure's web,
> the flag of fear I flew
> riding black stallions
> through the rocky streets.

These were a young writer's poems. In the main he recalled past epiphanic moments, but in 'The Long War' there was a deeper wisdom:

> death's family likeness in each face
> must show, at last, our brotherhood.

In their structure the poems were conventional, mostly organized in four- or six-line verses. 'A Moment of War', datelined 'Spanish Frontier, 1937', was a rare exception, with its irregular lines and versification, the use of exclamatory refrains – all suggesting gunfire – and its dramatic climax:

> your breathing is the blast, the bullet,
> and the final sky.

The title was to be revived nearly fifty years later for the third part of his autobiography.

Only one poem in the collection used rhyme. 'Deliverance' evoked the tramps and First World War deserters Laurie saw struggling to survive in Cotswold beechwoods when he was a child. The picture was of an unbalanced dying man, and the rhyme scheme added to its pathos:

> His sick veins now do spring alive,
> Leaves run along each bone,
> And in his hollow eyes the birds
> Sing out for him alone.

Many readers have wondered why these poems provide Laurie's only reference to the Second World War, barely mentioned in the story of his life. It may be that the Spanish war still dominated his thinking and drove out other personal reactions at the time or that, as his essays implied, life in London, however eventful, did not inspire him.

In the 1940s the portrait painter Anthony Devas and his family more or less adopted Laurie, who played the penniless poet for all he was worth. Nicolette Devas, in her autobiography *Two Flamboyant Fathers*, described how they first met Laurie at a party in Fulham. He was a romantic-looking young man 'with a thin, sensitive and sickly face' who looked like most people's idea of a poet. But, she discovered, 'There was a winter Laurie and a summer Laurie. During the winter he appeared poetically haggard, with bags under his eyes . . . at the first ray of spring sunshine he relaxed like a lizard and with closed eyes turned his face up to the sun.'[7]

She recalled how Laurie cajoled them into letting him lodge at the top of their house in Markham Square, Chelsea. Anthony and Nicolette Devas had three young children and she did not want a lodger who was also a friend, but Laurie persisted until she finally gave in: 'Laurie could charm the birds off the trees and the hind leg off a donkey.' He stayed with them for seven years, moving with them to Carlyle Square.

She remembered how during air raids in the 1940s the family, sheltering in the basement, were comforted by the strains of Laurie's violin coming from the top of the house – 'music from heaven, it seemed, between the guns and the bombs . . . Nowadays I never hear those violin pieces of Mozart without the echo of an air raid.' She felt that her husband did most of his best painting, and Laurie wrote many of his best poems, during this period. Anthony Devas painted a number of portraits of Laurie, whose face changed from day to day ('his weather was his moods'). One of these portraits now hangs in the National Portrait Gallery in London. Both men found strategies to calm their nerves. Laurie played the violin and recorder, but he also devised childish games such as flying paper aircraft on the roof. The poet Paul Potts lived in a basement opposite, and Laurie would aim a peashooter at him from his window. Very aptly the basement was known as Poet's Kitchen, where starving poets were fed by Elizabeth Smart, author of *By Grand Central Station I Sat Down and Wept*.

In June 1942 the Czech mining village of Lidice was razed to the ground by the Germans as a reprisal for the assassination of the Nazi security chief Reinhard Heydrich. All its surviving inhabitants, including children, were sent to concentration camps. British horror at the destruction of Lidice led to the formation of a Remember Lidice Group and the making of a film called *A Silent Village*. This was filmed by the Crown Film Unit in Wales, partly to draw parallels between Lidice and Welsh mining villages. Much moved by the Lidice story, Laurie put into verse an already translated poem, 'The Dead Village', on the same theme. 'The Dead Village', by the Czech poet Viktor Fischl, was published in Laurie's version in 1943 in London by the Young Czechoslovakia Press. It was a sixteen-page booklet illustrated by a Czech artist, Geza Szobel. Her uncompromising drawings showed the agony of men, women and children snatched from their shattered homes by brutal militaristic figures:

> It is no more, it is no more,
> the tongueless bells no longer ring,
> only the smoking walls remain.

The poem evoked the mutilated bodies of young women who once scrubbed floors and coalminers' shirts now stained with blood and ripped by bullets. The former life of the village was reflected in its desolate state:

> the doors without gossip,
> the lanes without lovers,
> the pitshafts where no hammers ring . . .
> the beer mugs no longer kiss together.

The damaged tools, the broken trees and the new growth of seeds speak of revenge – the trees would become gallows and the river would run with blood – but there was hope:

O tears of the dead village,
O dust of the dead village,
O glory of the living village!

Even in this translation one senses Laurie's preoccupation with the fused images of nature and death. It was a theme he would return to in the 1960s when the village school at Aberfan, a Welsh mining village, was engulfed by the collapse of an enormous coal tip. Perhaps as Laurie wrote about the destruction of Lidice, or the disaster at Aberfan, in his mind's eye he saw Slad.

As well as visiting their mother the Lee brothers kept in touch with their father, now retired and living with a married couple in the London suburb of Morden. Jack said: 'I think we visited our father once, twice at most. I remember him as artistic in the sense that he was a good musician, otherwise somewhat mean and pedantic. Neither Laurie nor I felt at ease with his *ménage à trois*. He was a cold man.'

Laurie told a similar story: 'Dear Dad, he was too prim ever to disappear completely. He joined the Civil Service and settled down with a very ugly woman and her husband in south London. I used to find them shredding cigarette ends into a tin to make roll-ups.'[8]

Reg died in 1942, aged sixty-five, while he was trying to start a car, according to Laurie. There is no record of which members of his family attended his funeral; some at least of the eight surviving sons and daughters must have been there. Laurie inherited from his father his musical talent and his fascination with beautiful women.

After the war Jack branched out into feature films – his most famous ones were to come in the 1950s – and Laurie transferred to the Green Park Film Unit and wrote scripts for films about tea in Assam, the Far East and Cyprus. Two of his early books, however, were nothing to do with films and all to do with the war in Europe. Between 1942 and 1945 he worked on a verse translation of 'The Dead Village' and wrote his official history of British wartime farming, *Land at War*. Here are two works so different it is hard to find anything in common. But the voice in both cases is a countryman's voice, the voice of one who loves nature the creator and passionately hates war the destroyer.

In 1950 Laurie's mother died in a nursing home in Painswick. Annie and her husband had never lived together after Reg joined the Army during the First World War, yet they never divorced. Laurie recorded in *Cider with Rosie* how it was. 'She had raised his two families, faithfully and alone: had waited thirty-five years for his praise. And through all that time she had clung to one fantasy – that aged and broken, at last in need, he might one day return to her. His death ended that promise and also ended her reason.'

Annie was buried, with all her family present, in Slad churchyard, near the grave of her four-year-old daughter Frances; and there, too, her celebrated son Laurie would be buried forty-seven years later. Her tombstone said simply: 'Annie Light. She loved this world.' Laurie paid remarkable tribute to her in a radio interview. He called her 'my scatty and brilliant, eccentric but fascinating madcap of a mother'. From her he had inherited his sense of fun and his unique imagination.

There can be no doubt that Annie was the greatest single influence on her son's development as a writer, and he acknowledged this often in articles and interviews. From her he acquired his appreciation of books, his sense of a good story and his love of life.

She was a collector and observer, and so was he – with the difference that she observed people and collected old china and items for her scrapbook, whereas Laurie stored up impressions of the natural world and vivid visual images. In his eighties he recalled how Annie and her children would sit by the fire in the old cottage: 'We all told each other stories in the kitchen corner. Now the mystery and imagination have been stolen; it's just satellite TV, quizzes and soap operas. But if there's a power failure, then you hear the old songs and stories. The ghosts come back by candlelight.'

Laurie went along with the Light family's belief that they had had remarkable forebears. 'Over there,' he said, pointing across the valley, 'they found a Bronze Age skeleton. I like to think it might have been an ancestor. My mother's people go back a long way around here.'

Above: Laurie at his stepsister Dorothy's wedding,
1927. Boys in front, from left to right: Laurie,
Tony and Jack. Middle row, from left to right:
Harold, the groom; Dorothy, the bride; the
groom's mother; Reg Lee, the bride's father;
Phyllis, the bridesmaid; and Laurie's mother,
Annie Lee

Right: Laurie in Morocco, 1948

Jan
love from
Laurie.
(The Desert Fox)

Sahara.

Clockwise from top left
Slad village from across the valley, as it is today;
Mrs Lee's Cottage, now called Rosebank;
Holy Trinity Church; Steanbridge Lake; the
former schoolteacher's house; next to the
schoolteacher's house the old village school

Jim Ruston

Facing page: The Woolpack Inn, Slad

Jim Ruston

Above: Laurie talking with Roy Fuller, the author and poet, at a party to celebrate the opening of the PEN Club's new headquarters in Chelsea, London, 1949

Hulton Getty

Left: Laurie, in his role as Curator of 'Eccentrics' Corner' and Caption-Writer-in-Chief at the Festival of Britain, demonstrates the talents of a guitar-playing toy hare, photographed in 1950

Hulton Getty

Clockwise from top left:

Laurie receives prize money from Dame Peggy Ashcroft for the W.H. Smith and Son second Annual Literary Award, 1960

Hulton Getty

Laurie and Kathy, 1960

Hulton Getty

Laurie judging a beauty contest, 1963

Mrs Eva Firth

Laurie relaxing with Kathy and Jessy as Christmas approaches, 1964

Hulton Getty

Above: The Queen's Elm, Fulham Road, Laurie's favourite pub in London for over twenty years. The regulars are, from left to right, Lord Valentine Thynne, the cartoonist Jak, Peter Owen, Laurie Lee, Kerry Hamilton, Marshall Pugh, Jan Kenny (later Treacy), Sean Treacy (landlord), Elisabeth Frink, Babs Craig, Bill Travers, Virginia McKenna, Dr Geoffrey Dove and William Thomson, 1976

Jan Treacy

Laurie promoting his books in Stroud, 1992

Joan Tucker

10
Farming Landscapes

Like a covered field you lie,
and remembering the exultant plough
your sheltered bosom stirs
and whispers warm with rain.

– 'Landscape'

IN the mid-1940s Laurie published the two books that most
directly seem to draw their energy from his farming ancestors. Fifty
years later he told an interviewer in Slad: 'We live close to our origins
here . . . This is no prefabricated landscape.' And farming, which he
knew and understood from early childhood, is at the heart of both
Land at War and *We Made a Film in Cyprus*.

His most specifically propagandist piece of writing for the Ministry
of Information was a review of Britain's agricultural industry through
five years of war. *Land at War* was subtitled *The Official Story of British
Farming 1939–1944*, and it was sold through the HMSO for one
shilling and sixpence. It profiled the radical changes in British farming
practice in the 1940s by presenting them as developments on a typical,
but imaginary, south of England farm. The farm may have been fictitious, but it carried a familiar name: an Abbey Farm lies just across the
Slad Valley from Laurie's childhood home. And it does not need much
imagination to link the parish details invented for the Ministry booklet to the real Abbey Farm or its neighbour, Knapp Farm, farmed for
generations by the Webbs, friends of the Lee family.

Years later Laurie was to record his affection for the Webbs: 'You
can look across and see Peter Webb's fields and his cows going in for
milking, and he's farming just as his father and grandfather did.' There
is little doubt that he looked to Knapp Farm for some of the source
material he used in *Land at War*.

Early on in the war a national survey, rather grandly heralded as another Domesday Book, set out to record the state of every farm in Britain. Laurie drew on this and superimposed upon it his personal knowledge of farming changes in the south Cotswolds. Through most of the war he visited his mother at Slad, called in at the Woolpack and discussed with old friends how the war was affecting them. Slad had its share of hardships: six local men died fighting and two other people were killed by a stray bombing raid on Painswick. The Cotswolds were targeted from time to time by bombers aiming at Gloucestershire's twenty-eight small airfields; and bombs were randomly jettisoned by German pilots returning from massive raids on Birmingham or Coventry.

But for Cotswold farmers, with most of the county given over to agriculture, the battle was to produce more and more food. The fictitious Abbey Farm turned 100 acres of arable and grass into 116 acres growing cereals and switched from mainly rearing poultry to breeding milk cows and some 200 pigs. Even the field names echo names well known in Slad: Woolpack, The Jungle, Gibbet, Badger Run and Sloe Meadow. Walkers through the Slad Valley today can pick out badger setts, hedges thick with sloes or a field with a view of the old gibbet site at Bulls Cross. A pictorial plan of the imaginary Abbey Farm land includes Woolpack Lane (Steanbridge Lane?) crossing a stream and what is recognizably the Stroud road through Slad. The buildings of Abbey Farm seem to be based on Steanbridge Farm, with pond, barns and orchards clearly marked. One can imagine Laurie on a weekend visit sketching out a lightly disguised plan of the Slad village farmland for his story of wartime British farming.

Of course it was no soulless ministerial document. It told a story, and Laurie enjoyed telling it. 'No weapon ever invented,' he began, 'is more deadly than hunger. It can spike guns, destroy courage and break the will of the most resolute peoples.' Then he plunged into a dramatic 1939 scenario of tumbledown buildings, rusting tools and weed-choked fields, sights familiar to him as a boy during the years of depression. The war had changed all that.

The first winter of the war was the coldest in living memory. Yet two million acres of old grassland were ploughed up for food production in a few months – 'the plough became another weapon of war; they ploughed by day and night – the land does not wait'. Horses began to be replaced everywhere by tractors shipped over from Canada, the United States and Australia. (These machines, Laurie noted, could harvest in a few hours twenty acres which had previously taken a week.)

It is possible to imagine Laurie Lee, countryman to the core, plodding through mountains of Ministry of Agriculture statistics and breathing life into them for this report. Not for him dull lists of tractors and turnips. He swept the reader through acres of daffodils in Devon and Cornwall prosaically converted to wheat, carrots and onions. He conjured up the ancient apple orchards of Cambridgeshire newly occupied by cows and potatoes.

Cereals and potatoes were the main wartime food crops, and almost every farmer was obliged to grow a quota of potatoes. This was not popular. Laurie told a tale of a Cotswold sheep farmer who was told to plant ten acres of potatoes without benefit of special planting equipment. '"I heard a noise like a gurt clock," says a neighbour. "Then I seen old Jesse. He'd got a three-furrow plough he was ridin' on, and a tin bath full of spuds in his arms. He'd raked up an old chimney-pot from somewhere and got it wedged between his knees. There was some sort of gadget stuck on the wheel which rang a bell every time it turned round, and each time this bell rang old Jesse dropped a tater down the chimney . . . he was ploughing three furrows and planting at the same time, dropping the tater in the third furrow and so a-pacing out the rows."'

It is possible that Laurie heard this tale in the Woolpack or the Butchers' Arms or the Carpenters' Arms. Graphically he described the struggles of farmers unused to dairy farming who were required to produce milk. Cattle needed care and attention whatever day it was. In winter the farmer had to be up long before sunrise. At calving time he had to be up all night. The farmer milked twice a day, dawn and afternoon. He had to wash down each animal, feed it, milk it, clean the shed, clean himself up and ensure the purity of the milk. Dairy farmers, Laurie pointed out, did not do all this for love or just for money. Their work was real war service. Probably he watched the milking at one of the Slad farms, asked questions, built up his own picture of farm life.

And so, too, when he described the talk of farmers at a War Agricultural Committee meeting, Laurie Lee would watch and listen. He found their phrases short, to the point, falling on the ear like proverbs or blank verse quotations: 'Never touch that field after Christmas'; 'Ground's too cold'; 'Cold as my grandmother.'

A whole section of *Land at War* was devoted to the story of the Women's Land Army, the 90,000 women who worked during the war on farms – some for only eighteen shillings a week plus their keep. He summed up their contribution in what could almost be a poem:

> This young sun-tanned, green-sweatered, cord-breeched army was throughout the war in the forefront of the battle. They figured in every ordeal and triumph wartime farming had to offer. They came from shops, offices, beauty parlours, dancing schools. They went wherever they were needed, did any job that would replace a man. They have known six winters and six summers on the land, have gathered in six wartime harvests.

Land at War ended with a eulogy to the volunteers, schoolchildren and others, who worked on the land during their vacations. When they got back to their desks, counters and work-benches, blistered and burnt red by the sun, he surmised, their food tasted better, they had a new understanding of country life and, above all, 'the farmer's life seemed more real to them, less of a fable, because they had shared it with him. Surely the gulf that has hitherto existed between the two communities, town and country, could be bridged in no better way?'

From bleak British fields in the coldest winter of the century Laurie turned his attention to the hot and sunny olive groves and orchards of Cyprus. Published in 1947, *We Made a Film in Cyprus* was the record of an immensely happy visit to Cyprus in 1945 for the Crown Film Unit. Coming immediately after *Land at War,* the contrast in farming styles must have been breathtaking: from intensive mechanized food production to a poor peasant economy.

The slim, well-illustrated book was dedicated 'To the People of Cyprus', and Laurie wrote in a brief preface: 'This book is a souvenir of a documentary film made in Cyprus during the last days of the European war. The film was first shown in 1946 at the Curzon Cinema, London. It has since been exhibited at two international film festivals, in France and Czechoslovakia.'

It was one of his most successful creative efforts for the Ministry of Information. As scriptwriter he collaborated with the cameraman, Ralph Keene, both in making the film and writing the book. The result, although government sponsored, was a perceptive and personal account of the island of Cyprus and its people under British rule. It also outlined the complications of making an official film on a shoestring budget, and it revealed Laurie at his happiest – on a working holiday.

The project began, Laurie recorded, when he met Ralph in a London pub and learned that he was off to Cyprus to make a film. 'Well, I got him into a corner and gave him some weak beer, and bullied him, and boasted of my knowledge of the place. And in the end I was signed up to go too, and write the story.'

At the beginning of *We Made a Film in Cyprus* Laurie explained that he had spent just a few weeks in Cyprus before the war, when he was exploring the Mediterranean on tramp steamers (he had visited Beirut, Cypus and Cairo between 1938 and 1939). But the Ministry was suitably impressed and authorized him to buy bush shirts and a drill suit (still *de rigueur* for colonial administrators in the 1940s). Thus attired, Laurie set off on a two-day flight via Cairo – a disappointing journey after his previous leisurely four-week trip to the island by sea. The plan was for him to spend seven days ahead of the camera crew, plotting a script ready for shooting. Cyprus was at that time a Crown Colony, and Laurie's brief was to present some of the benefits of colonial government.

It was an official business visit, constrained by time, by the demands of the island's excessively keen young government information officer and by the need to find good film locations and amateur actors in a very short space of time. But Laurie, poet and countryman, reacted with an outburst of inspired words to everything he saw. The island and its people enchanted him, and they responded to him. Lemon trees laden with fruit made him think of the udders of cows needing to be milked. Silkworms sleeping in nests of mulberry leaves reminded him of the millions of miles of silk thread they had provided for barrage balloons defending London in air raids – the balloons to him were gargantuan replicas of the silkworm cocoons.

He saw the Abbey of Bellapais (later to inspire Laurence Durrell's *Bitter Lemons*) as 'white and fragile, like a picked bone'. Goats, allowed to roam free, had withered the olive trees and dwarfed the pines. They stared with 'pale, cold pagan eyes'. He watched a man throw a bucketful of fish over mosquitoes as a deterrent. In a dark monastery a sunburst of brass sprang to life among the icons. In Nicosia he sampled the nightlife and found it boring, but the markets of the capital delighted him. The narrow streets resembled a maze, and craftsmen in their workshops offered him their greetings. The monastery of Kykko produced scent from thousands of roses, 'a distillation of all summers'.

A small drama was staged by Laurie and some villagers. They brought him a violin and he played, improvising, while men of the village acted out a gruesome dagger dance symbolizing murder. One dancer leaned back until he could grip with his teeth a dagger plunged in the ground, then mimed the act of stabbing and skinning another dancer. Laurie picked up the tune as best he could, 'in gusts of wine and garlic'.

Places provided drama, too. On Easter Sunday he reached the ancient port of Famagusta, immortalized by another English poet, James Elroy Flecker. Petals of poppies flew across the road like butterflies, and a forest of windmills rattled in the breeze. By now Laurie had written his first draft and needed to find his actors. In Famagusta, on the last day allotted for scriptwriting, he found them: Vassos, a goatherd, and Nikos, a farmer, naturals to play the roles of typical Cypriots. A bond grew up between them and Laurie – they called him Lavrendius. If he had not met them the film would have been stillborn.

On Easter Monday two cameramen flew in to Nicosia from Cairo to join him, and together they watched a baptism, village sports and a film show in the town square. As the entire community waited for the flickering pictures on the white sheet which provided an improvised screen, a man came running down the street, shouting. The war in Europe was over. The locals clapped and celebrated, although, as Laurie pointed out, it meant little to them. In Nicosia the night was given over to drinking, dancing and the sound of bells.

Laurie's script was finished and it was almost time to leave Cyprus. He lay awake listening to the bells, reflecting not so much on the government propaganda film as on the film he would have liked to have made, about real Cypriots, about their poverty and about their strange traditions.

The second part of the book was Ralph's account of the filming, illustrated mainly with his own photographs. However, one picture shows the two men after swimming at Cape Andreas: Ralph the cynic, smoking and looking detached, while Laurie sits on a rock playing his recorder. Elsewhere he appears in a safari suit and long woollen socks, apparently fast asleep on a mountain of oranges.

Ralph clearly felt that Laurie had got the best of the deal. 'The scenario said "Shoot this, shoot that" but not how it was to be done. That was my job, while Laurie could lie back in the sun, eating apricots and oranges and playing his shepherd's pipe.' Laurie, he complained, did not allow for lighting difficulties. When Ralph pointed out that a church cross was in darkness, Laurie would merely suggest that a convenient shaft of sunlight might solve the problem. Strong sun affected the film negatives, so all the film stock had to be rushed back to London in a diplomatic bag. The goats were uncooperative. Language differences got in the way of instructions to the farmer and the goatherd. None the less, despite Ralph's anxieties and Laurie's laid-back approach, the film was shot in thirty-eight days, and the English film makers left behind many Cypriot friends.

The book ended with the working script, and Laurie's voice can plainly be heard: 'Out of this sea rose the Grecian Aphrodite, in this place was her legendary beauty born. And the water of the sea fell from her body and became flowers. And they called her the Goddess of Love . . . FADE OUT Cypriot song (sung by a single male voice) and FADE IN historical music, from Petro Petrides Greek Suite.'

To modern ears the commentary sounds somewhat dated, even stilted and complacent. But even without visual accompaniment it does not take much imagination to see the young scriptwriter scanning the dry and barren landscape, his eye lighting here and there on scenes of pure magic – the village of limestone houses 'as solid and square as any village in the Cotswolds', where girl lace-makers stitched in cool green courtyards, the vultures like 'bent black metal wheeling over pine trees'.

He imbibed the sun, the music, the personality of the island and sat in innumerable cafés drinking red wine with his new friends or playing his pipe in a monastery garden. Cyprus provided a new source of inspiration and gave rise to new poems.

11

Laurie the Playwright

Tonight has no moon,
No food for the pilgrim;
the fruit tree is bare,
the rose bush a thorn
and the ground bitter with stones.

– 'Christmas Landscape'

L AURIE'S second poetry collection, *The Bloom of Candles*, appeared in
1947, the same year as *Peasants' Priest*, a verse play for the Canterbury Festival. The poems and the play shared a certain wistfulness, as
if the maturing writer, now aged thirty-three, was preoccupied with
more melancholy aspects of his world view. Death, harsh winter and
man's inhumanity to man were dominant among the themes.

The title of this second book was taken from a line in 'Christmas
Landscape' ('And the fir tree warms to a bloom of candles') where the
paradox of Christmas was summed up in the final lines:

In the blood of our grief
the cold earth is suckled . . .
. . . in the last cry of anguish
the child's first breath is born.

A similar mood ran through 'The Wild Trees' ('torn branches of
brick and steel frozen against the sky') and the grieving couplets of
'Poem for Easter'. Even the startling images of sunrise in 'The Edge of
Day' conveyed a message of death in life ('Lit by the heart's exploding
sun,/Bursting from night to night').

It was an abiding disappointment to Laurie, and to students of his
verse, that he was less well known as a poet than as a teller of tales.
Certainly critics recognized his worth. The historian C.V. Wedgwood
wrote: 'The more startling or fanciful the vision, the more firm and

exact the words in which it is expressed. At his best he involves the reader with him completely in the intensity of the captured moment.'

As well as hinting at an obsession with death (seen in images of Easter, Christmas, a dead fox) *The Bloom of Candles* brought together those Lee poems which collectively reflect the drama of the four seasons, the wildlife and the moods of the Cotswold valleys.

In 'First Love' a boy, 'confused in his day's desire', equated his early sexual longings with the thrill of night fishing or woodland hunting. 'April Rise', one of the best loved of Laurie's poems, drew on the image of a girl among swans to personify spring. 'Field of Autumn' (a poem that Laurie often read in public) and 'Thistle' looked ahead from the riches of summer and autumn to the coming of snow and the land-scape ghosts of the year.

'Day of These Days' and 'On Beacon Hill' were lyrical hymns to young love in summer ('arching, our bodies gather light'), while 'Cock-Pheasant' captured the essence of this beautifully plumed bird. Other poems recalled Laurie's times in Cyprus, Spain and in India – he visited Assam to make a propaganda film for the tea industry, *A Tale in a Tea Cup*, in 1947 – but the heart of the book was in its view of the world encapsulated in a Gloucestershire valley.

Several critics have observed that he wrote poetry to be spoken aloud rather than read. Others draw attention to the Gloucestershire speech rhythms in his verse, as well as his sensuality and emotional observation of detail. In his third decade he had established himself as a published poet and had turned to another form of expression: drama.

Laurie's second major publication in 1947 was a verse play. Verse drama had fallen out of fashion in the eighteenth century and with a few exceptions (Shelley's *Prometheus Unbound*, Thomas Hardy's *The Dynasts*) it remained so until T.S. Eliot and Christopher Fry rein-vented the genre in the 1930s and 1940s. *The Cocktail Party, Murder in the Cathedral* and *The Lady's Not for Burning* were all successful in the West End. A number of plays written partly in verse, partly in prose came to be associated with cathedrals and churches, so seeming to revive the cult of medieval mystery plays.

Laurie was commissioned by the Friends of Canterbury Cathedral to write a verse drama for the Canterbury Festival of 1947. It was to be acted by amateurs in the cathedral itself and it was decided that the play should deal with the Peasants' Revolt of 1381. The six-scene play was published in 1947 by H. J. Goulden in an acting edition for the Festival of the Friends of Canterbury Cathedral.

The play is reminiscent in mood of *Murder in the Cathedral*. Eliot's play was commissioned for the 1935 festival by the Bishop of Chichester, later well known for his part in seeking British government support for the German generals plotting against Hitler. (There is some piquancy in relating Archbishop Becket's stand against Henry II to Bishop Bell's championship of the anti-Hitler plot in Germany.)

The Canterbury Festival was suspended during the war years, when the cathedral was the victim of German bombing raids. Laurie's play was the first post-war festival commission after the building's restoration. Christopher Fry's *Thor, With Angels*, followed in 1948; his setting was a Kentish Anglo-Saxon farmstead in AD 596, immediately before the coming of St Augustine who built the first church at Canterbury. So all three of the Canterbury verse plays dealt with the early and often tragic history of Christianity in Kent.

Christopher Fry maintained a lifelong friendship with Laurie, and at the age of ninety he read a poem in memory of his old friend at Laurie's memorial service. The same year he wrote in a letter: 'What I should know about, but alas don't, is the play he wrote for the Canterbury Festival at the cathedral . . . I think he did it the year after the one I did in 1948 . . . I looked forward eagerly to meeting Laurie and Kathy each year at the West Country Writers' Congress; though our meetings were rather brief and infrequent, they were always warm and good fun.'[1]

Peasants' Priest predated another drama in blank verse by Christopher Fry. This was *A Sleep of Prisoners*, involving four contemporary imprisoned soldiers, first performed in 1951 at the University Church, Oxford.

One can view these four plays as representing a sudden flowering of English poetic drama in and around the Second World War. Starved of new plays during the war, theatre in England welcomed what was almost a new genre. T. S. Eliot, Christopher Fry and Laurie all went on to write more verse plays, although these were no longer inspired by church history or a church context. *Peasants' Priest* had its roots in a long and honourable tradition of popular plays performed in or around churches. These were the very beginnings of English theatre, originating in the Latin Mass of the early Middle Ages. From the thirteenth century onwards miracle plays re-enacted the Liturgy or familiar Bible stories such as Noah's Flood, gradually leading on to the great vernacular mystery plays of the trade guilds. These were performed annually at the feast of Corpus Christi in Chester, Coventry, York, Wakefield and other cathedral cities. Canterbury appears not to have had a medieval mystery cycle.

Laurie turned for his festival celebration to a landmark in English history. The so-called Peasants' Revolt sprang from a crippling poll tax imposed in 1379 to counteract rising wages paid to farmworkers in the years after the Black Death. Riots broke out all over England, but particularly in Essex, where they were led by Wat Tyler, and in Kent, where they were led by John Balle (or Ball). Canterbury was sacked and the rebels marched on London, demanding an end to serfdom. They managed to seize the Tower of London. When Wat Tyler was stabbed to death by the Lord Mayor of London the rebellion ended; but the young King Richard II surrendered to the mob and made tax concessions, which were later revoked.

Before the revolt John Balle, known as 'the mad priest of Kent', had been imprisoned and excommunicated for disagreeing publicly with the Archbishop of Canterbury. When the rebellion collapsed he fled to Coventry, was recaptured and executed. Here was a folk hero for Laurie to build his play around; moreover a Kentish folk hero and a churchman who believed in social equality and preached it to the day of his death. Nothing could be more appropriate for Canterbury in the post-war days of 1947.

Several of the characters were historical, but others appear to be products of Laurie's imagination: among them Barfoot, an escaped serf; Flint, an ex-soldier; Skelp, an outlaw; Martha, a tavern girl; and Bowman, a rebel.

The play opened with a prologue spoken by Yellow Mask and Green Mask, *commedia dell'arte* figures. The mood of the main characters, the rebel recruits, was articulated by Skelp describing the horrors of the Black Death, which had halved the population of the Kent countryside. Skelp launched into an attack on the poll tax:

> For every new-fledged fleet sunk by the French
> another poll tax falls upon our heads.
> For every town they burn, there falls a flock
> of clerks, like soot, to choke the peasant's throat.
> One army dies in France. Another, here,
> armed with quill-pens, scratches for widow's pence.

Next the audience witnessed John Balle in prison arguing with a reactionary friar, his gaoler, using the imagery of one brought up in the country:

> I knew you as a boy
> running in rags about your father's hut.
> I've seen you weep red-eyed among the reeds,
> mourning a weasled swan.
> None was so swift as you to uncage a falcon, loose a netted hare.

Later the mother of the boy king Richard II would tell him in the Tower of London of 'heads on posts at crossroads grinning red like turnip lanterns'. Laurie may well have been recalling such lanterns from his Cotswold boyhood, part of the same life of the village as the mills and flocks he saw down the road:

> The miller's flour ground small
> Shall feed our lack.
> The Shepherd's rag of wool
> Shall ride our back.

Eventually the audience saw John Balle standing on Blackheath preaching under a banner, a passionate demagogue urging his peasant followers to march on the city, where Wat Tyler has already seized London Bridge. A rural image coloured Yellow Mask's summing up of the last few hours of the courtiers trapped in the Tower: 'The rich sun drips from summer's heavy husk, and night's delirium ends.'

Peasants' Priest is brief and suitable for inclusion as part of a pageant. As verse drama to be staged in a cathedral, celebrating a major historical event particular to that place, it works well, with the storming of the Tower of London the play's dramatic climax. It was the first of Laurie Lee's verse dramas to be acted and published.

Meanwhile his social life was expanding, centred on the Colony Room in Soho and various Chelsea watering holes. Here he met kindred spirits and enjoyed drinking sessions – when he could afford it. These were the years of poverty, and he acquired something of a reputation for not always buying a round when it was his turn.

A glimpse of Laurie comes from someone who met him on holiday in Kent when he shared a seaside cottage with the Devases and Norman Hepple (later president of the Royal Society of Portrait Painters). Stephanie Thompson, widow of the novelist Leo Walmsley and daughter of the newspaper humourist whose pseudonym was Nathaniel Gubbins, remembered meeting Laurie in a seafront café in Deal. 'I think it was 1947. My friend Margaret said: "Look, there's Laurie Lee the poet", and he made me feel very grand when he said "Ah, the illustrious Miss Gubbins." It was a café where you could get eggs and bacon and toast for tenpence. My parents were friendly with Anthony Devas and his family, and the London visitors all used to rent a fisherman's cottage near the harbour.'

At about this time Jack Lee was making a name for himself nationally as a film director – and as a cricketer. In 1947 he made *The Woman in the Hall,* followed by his first film set in Australia, *Once a Jolly Swagman*. Three years later came a great box-office success, *The Wooden Horse,* which he co-directed. Laurie was at the première and basked in the reflected glory of his older brother.

Jack joined the élite Lord's Taverners – cricketers mainly from the world of show business who raised money for charity by playing against club sides – and took his own eleven each summer down to his old home in Gloucestershire. World-class players who turned out at Sheepscombe included Keith Miller, Ben Barnett and Farouk Engineer. Laurie was never a player, but there are stories of him playing his fiddle in the pub after a game and taking London friends to see village cricket matches.

Living and working in London in the late 1940s Laurie gradually became one of the literati, a familiar figure at book events and a member of the Garrick Club, popular with actors and writers. A contemporary noted at this time: 'With his floppy handkerchiefs and fizzy-bright jackets he was rather more Arts Club dandy than Gloucestershire yokel. The Garrick Club tie was also often in evidence.' Home was a series of attic flats in Chelsea and he wrote whatever he was commissioned to write.[2]

Thus he found himself writing for radio, an entirely new medium for him. He had been commissioned in 1946 to write a play for the BBC's Third Programme. It was broadcast that year, although it did not appear in print until 1948. The Third Programme was conceived as a station for broadcasting an innovative mixture of music, verse and prose. Laurie was one of the new generation of post-war poets invited to contribute. He came up with the story of 'man's first voyage round the world, a stumbling achievement as revolutionary to the human mind, perhaps, as anything that has ever happened to it'. He called it *The Voyage of Magellan: A Dramatic Chronicle for Radio,* and in his introductory note to the printed version he wrote of it as an 'essay in reduction', compressing three years of travel into an hour, the breadth of the Pacific into a one-minute speech and Magellan's crew of 250 into a chorus of four, plus the storyteller.

Laurie demonstrated a good understanding of radio's potential as well as its constraints. Portuguese music, church bells, the repetitive rhythms of Latin prayer and emotive sound effects – the trickling of water imagined by shipwrecked sailors – all were brought into play behind the agonized dialogue of seamen dying, killing, being killed.

There was no attempt to rely on howling winds or the crash of waves, clichés, even then, of radio sound effects. Laurie created his drama mainly through the narrative voice of the sailor who related the story of Magellan to a blind beggar. He explained his intention: 'Written for radio, it plans to transmit above all else a visual experience, and for this reason the story is told to a blind beggar, with whom the radio listener is identified.'

The play opened in Seville, where the eighteen survivors of Magellan's crew had come to do penance for sins committed on the other side of the world. Listeners heard voice after voice listing the huge quantities of stores taken on board Magellan's five ships in 1519. Later the ships' names were supplied: the *Trinidad*, the *San Antonio*, the *Santiago*, the *Concepción*, and the *Victoria*. Watching was a Portuguese spy, Alvarez, reporting to the king of Portugal on the activities of a compatriot he saw as a traitor, setting out from Spain to seek the riches of the New World.

The sailor recounted how the five ships floated like acorns across the Atlantic, with Magellan as a black sea-beetle in command:

> We did not love Magellan,
> he was sharp as pepper, hard as a turtle,
> crafty, bloody, cold as pitch . . .
> he drove us through seas no keel has cut before,
> and when we thought we'd reached the end of the world
> he looked over the horizon and saw that it was the beginning.

Music and the terrified cries of sailors conveyed the horrors of the voyage, storm, bitter cold, mutiny, the three months of sailing the Pacific with no sight of land and food supplies exhausted. Men went mad, died from ghastly sicknesses, were thrown – or threw themselves – overboard. Finally the survivors landed on an island with friendly inhabitants, some of whom they baptized, but then sailed on to a hostile island where Magellan was killed by a poisoned arrow. Only a few of the sailors escaped in two of the ships and drifted to the Spice Islands, where some chose to settle. Some two dozen only sailed for home in one ship, the *Victoria*. They drifted to Mozambique, rounded the Cape of Good Hope and so returned home to Spain – not woulin triumph but in shame and remorse, as the narrator admitted to the beggar.

Inevitably there were reminders of Coleridge's *Ancient Mariner* and of tales of Columbus in the play. But to these resonances Laurie added a personal knowledge of Catholic Spain, a perception of hardships at sea and, above all, a poet's ear:

> The fingers of these girls are like streams of water,
> lighter than swallows touching the strings of fountains.
> O Paradise in the harps of their fingers
> and their bodies crouching like settled doves!

The verse is full of vivid imagery:

> At last my sails are full!
> See how they tug the heavens,
> taking great gulps of air
> like slaves new freed from jail.

Doom is foreshadowed in the narrator's portrait of Magellan:

> You would have seen a man shot through with luck and evil.
> In the blazing months of that Seville summer
> he hobbled among those ships
> preparing his doom and glory.
> Each thread of sail he tested for his shroud.

In October 1946 the BBC gave *The Voyage of Magellan* an impressive first broadcast, with the producer Rayner Heppenstall as its midwife, music specially composed by Brian Easedale and with an all-star cast. Magellan was played by the distinguished Shakespearian actor Frederick Valk and the sailor-narrator by Bernard Miles.

Two years later the play was published by Laurie's former editor, John Lehmann, with illustrations by Edward Burra. In the introductory note Laurie Lee called *The Voyage of Magellan* an experiment in radio drama. The world that Magellan circumnavigated was another world from ours, he stressed. And Magellan's sailors were 'Mediterranean strangers, brutal, sensitive and deeply religious'. The abiding memory left by the play was of almost unendurable hardship, cruelty and burning ambition. Laurie summed up the sailors' experience: 'The shape of the play is the shape of its story, a circle.'

For a year or two after this Laurie spent his time writing poetry and short articles, a happy Bohemian about London, making occasional forays to Gloucestershire. In a broadcast essay he admitted, however, that London never truly became his home: 'For years I have lived in the flats, rooms and garrets of this city, the drawers in the human filing-cabinets that stand in blank rows down the streets of Kensington and Notting Hill. Yet when I talk of home I still think of that damp green valley near Stroud where I was brought up.' The boys he went to school with, bald now and married, would scarcely recognize him, he guessed. 'Take a train home, go to the pub, hand round cigarettes and remark that you've just been made Chief Inspector of Inkwells at the Ministry of Boil and Trouble' and their reaction – he conjectured – would be to tell a parish tale about a champion rabbit poacher.[3]

So why, he asked himself, did he stay in London? He enjoyed the 'mass gregariousness', the city atmosphere of autumn afternoons and winter nights, the warmth and noise of fish shops, singing on buses. As always he selects with a poet's eye, a musician's ear. And yet: 'Here in London I am like a radio receiver set up in a cellar . . . I can lie here in bed in the morning and know exactly what kind of day it is a hundred miles away; that there is frost on the fruit bloom, or . . . the sheep will be tumbled into the sheepwash and bleating under the shears.'

The Cotswolds were in his blood. London remained a cage with its door open, but he could not leave. The cage was comfortable enough and there were things he wanted to do; but he knew, and the reader knew, that he would not stay long.

From time to time he travelled, scripting a film about India, visiting Mexico, Poland, Italy, Morocco, the Caribbean. Outlets for his traveller's tales included the BBC, *Encounter*, the *New York Times Book Review*, *Vogue* and the *Geographical Magazine*. The best of these essays were later collected and published in 1975 under the title *I Can't Stay Long*. One of these was a lyrical account of a flight on Concorde.

He was a restless observer of landscapes and the human condition. Much of what he saw he stored away to be written about years later, with hindsight, wisdom and emotion recollected if not in tranquillity at least in a state of distanced equilibrium. His observation emerged as poetry or a form of autobiography perhaps unique to him: what he called a scrapbook of loves and obsessions and of places he rejoiced to have known 'before jet-tourism and war finished off most of them'.

And then came the 1950s, with marriage, acceptance into the honoured establishment and a return to his roots.

12

Anni Mirabili: The 1950s

> I, with as easy hunger, take
> entire my season's dole;
> welcome the ripe, the sweet, the sour,
> the hollow and the whole.
>
>   – 'Apples'

THE 1950s were a very good time for Laurie's personal life and career. He married Katherine Francesca Polge at Kensington Register Office on 17 May 1950. She was that same girl who had sat on his lap in Provence in 1936, when he was on his way back from Spain, and announced her intention of marrying him. He described her much later (in *Two Women*, published in 1983) as a chubby five-year-old who spoke a French dialect he could not understand.

Katherine – usually known as Kathy or Cathy – was the daughter of Jean Baptiste Polge, an artist, sailor, fisherman and bullfighter, friend of the poet Roy Campbell, the sculptor Epstein and other British expatriates living at Martigues on the outskirts of Marseilles in the 1930s. Jean Baptiste, who was part French, part Swedish, had married into the British expatriate community. When war broke out, his wife, born Helen Garman, took her ten-year-old daughter to London and worked there for the Free French forces. In 1942 Jean Baptiste was killed serving as a gunner in the French Navy, and his widow later married an Italian lawyer, Mario Sarfatti.

Helen belonged to a remarkable family. Five of the seven Garman sisters were extraordinary: gifted artistically, beautiful and inclined to form relationships with men of rare talent. Helen was to become Laurie's mother-in-law. Mary was the wife of Roy Campbell. Kathleen became the second wife of the sculptor Jacob Epstein, after a long relationship with him. Sylvia was reputed to be the only woman ever to become close to Lawrence of Arabia. Lorna had been Laurie's lover, was wife of a publisher and the mother of Laurie's daughter Jasmine (now Yasmin). One brother, Douglas, was a poet. The head of the Garman dynasty was a wealthy doctor from the Midlands, Walter Garman, and their mother was the illegitimate daughter of a peer.

The Garman sisters run like a thread through Laurie's life, and Kathy Lee has said that they deserve a book to themselves; indeed, they figure prominently in the biographies of the men connected with the family. The most newsworthy was Kathleen, who left home at nineteen to study music in London, became a talented pianist and met Jacob Epstein in 1921. They had several children together but did not marry until 1955, some years after his first wife's death. One daughter married Lucien Freud, another lived with the artist Mark Joffé, father of the film director Roland Joffé.

During the war members of the extended Epstein family grouped and regrouped in each other's homes. Kathy, daughter of Helen, lived for a time with her aunt Kathleen and several of Epstein's children, while her mother did war work. After the war she remembers Laurie visiting them and playing piano and violin duets with her accomplished aunt – one of many indications that Laurie was indeed a talented musician.

This was the remarkable clan that Laurie married into in 1950 and grew to know over the years – so well that he was entrusted by them to write a commentary on Epstein's work and the foreword to Roy Campbell's memoirs.

The architect and art critic Stephen Gardiner knew Laurie and Kathy and Helen in the 1950s through the Epsteins. 'Kathy once said that there were many fine sculptors around; they were the priests, Epstein was God.'[1] He met the Lees at parties held at the home of another close friend of Laurie's, Elisabeth Frink, the sculptor, who lived in the flat below him. 'He sometimes played his violin for us. He loved women enormously. There was a time when he was in hospital with a hernia and was surrounded by girl-friends. He was said to be a bit of a snob who liked titled people. We also used to meet in Italy, where Kathy often visited her mother and Mario Sarfatti at their villa on Lake Garda.'[2]

Stephen Gardiner admired Laurie's poems ('the quartzy way he put words together') and thought highly of his perceptions of Jacob Epstein's work. He quotes Laurie's comment on *Ecce Homo*, the extraordinary figure carved from exceptionally hard marble in 1935: 'Squat, square, the totem of our crimes, he stands before us in a pitiless, blinding light . . . ten thousand churchfuls of sentimentalised Christs are denied for ever by this raw and savage figure.'

In his biography of Jacob Epstein Stephen Gardiner told a strange tale of Helen Polge and the very young Kathy, who had been sent for wartime safety to stay with the oldest Garman, Sylvia, in her Dorset cottage. This was near the home of T.E. Lawrence, Lawrence of Arabia, who had been killed in a motor-cycle accident in 1935. Sylvia owned a portrait of Lawrence painted by Augustus John – Lawrence had also been the inspiration for Jacob Epstein's *Lucifer* – and Helen believed that there had been a supernatural visitation by the dead Lawrence while she was staying at the cottage.

Kathy went to school in London and travelled after the war with her mother to Martigues, Florence and elsewhere, thus becoming multi-lingual. Laurie met her again as a schoolgirl; their paths crossed on the fringe of a post-war Chelsea arts community not unrelated to that idyllic pre-war colony in Marseilles.

He escorted her around London and to the seaside and became more and more drawn to her 'clear gold beauty and . . . eyes huge as picture windows'. During one of Kathy's Italian visits, when she was not quite eighteen, he sent a telegram to Florence asking her mother's consent to their marriage. He was surprised when she said yes. Early in 1950 he met Kathy at Victoria Station and installed her in a tiny flat in Collingham Place, near Earls Court Station, with two rooms and a kitchen. 'Her cooking was primitive, and we both lost weight,' he later recalled.

Within three months they were married. The groom was described as 'Bachelor, Writer'; his father Reginald Joseph as 'deceased retired executive, Customs and Excise, wines and spirits'. The witnesses were Cecil Day-Lewis and Jill Balcon, soon to be married themselves. It was a quiet, private event, with the bride carrying a spray of lilies, followed by lunch in Soho where the waiters treated Kathy as a queen. Afterwards Laurie went back to his Ministry of Information office, unable to afford any more time off.

At the time of their wedding Laurie was not quite thirty-six and Kathy just eighteen. She had been brought up in a cosmopolitan community and was at home with people in the arts world. Laurie described himself as 'a known bachelor' who had set his face against a long-term commitment; a civil servant not yet ready to strike out and earn his living by writing. The age gap did not seem to matter at all, nor did the next decade of poverty. A devoted couple, they remained happily married for forty-seven years.

What did surprise Laurie's old friends was that the professional bachelor, the perennial lover (one who had known him for years called him 'quite a philanderer'), should settle down so completely. It did not seem in character. Yet Laurie had always been susceptible to lovely women.

Here was one remarkably beautiful woman, re-entering his life after a decade, whom Laurie could not resist. Yet he had little, at first, to offer Kathy. When he gave up his job to become a full-time writer they moved to two bare rooms in a war-ravaged part of Chelsea and lived on spaghetti. They had to manage on £200 a year and relied for decent meals on better-off married friends. These, he said, were sad, empty days for Kathy, and Laurie preferred living away from London, but they waited for better times.

Soon after their marriage they returned to Laurie's old pre-war haunts in Spain to revisit Almuñécar and look for surviving friends from the days that he had spent there as a hotel violinist. The search, and the gradual recognition that Spain had changed almost beyond belief in such a short time, are poignantly described in *A Rose for Winter*, published some years later, which was subtitled *Travels in Andalusia* and dedicated to 'Kathy and the Benefactor'. One critic said it communicated 'that electric thrill that comes only from Spain'. Laurie wrote that it took less than five minutes for the sights and sounds and smells to wipe out fifteen years and take him back to the day when he had walked in from Cádiz with his violin on his back and paid threepence a night to sleep on straw near the mules. But of course it was not the same town he had known, and people were reluctant to talk about the past, especially the Civil War.

However, the men loved Kathy (Kati, he calls her here), sang love songs to her and welcomed them both. They travelled through much of southern Spain on this extended honeymoon, and the book is full of their mutual admiration and happiness. A vivid account of a bullfight in Seville reminds the reader that Laurie was at heart a countryman, with more empathy towards the bulls than most of the Spanish crowd. One bull walked into the ring 'sadly as a lost calf'. And 'if ever a body lacked a vocation for martyrdom, this bull was it . . . all he wished was to be back in the brown pastures under Medina'. The Andalusian bulls recalled the sleepy brown heifers of Slad farms or the handsome bullocks coming under the auctioneer's hammer at Gloucester Cattle Market.

Landscapes were still the mainspring of his writing. Second in importance only to the Cotswolds comes the Andalusian coastline between Málaga and Almería. Almuñécar (his so-called Castillo) still moved him deeply. In the Middle Ages it had been a pirate stronghold, a fortress on a rock guarded by sea and mountains. Now he found the estuary silted up and growing poor-quality sugar-cane, the castle in ruins and the town desolate, 'stripped of its Barbary jewels'. The ragged shoreline was littered with broken boats, and the hotel where he had enjoyed life so much seemed full of ghosts. The more he explored, the more Laurie saw to depress him. A whole generation of Almuñécar's men had disappeared in the Civil War. Cafés were abandoned, the town fountain filled with litter, and goats browsed in the gardens. The mountains struck him as 'sharp and jagged, like a cordon of police'. The disillusion of coming back to a much-loved, much-changed place parallels the disillusion of the idealist grown older.

He slept badly and watched the fishermen at dawn, day after day, hauling in half-empty nets. He still imagined in their salty eyes 'a savage past, an inglorious present and a future choked with unmentionable hopes'. What he could not know was that within a few decades Almuñécar would discover a new prosperity, buoyed up by waves of northern European tourists. And as time passed and his books sold he would be seen as an early champion of the attractions of the town.

The final landscape of southern Spain in *A Rose for Winter* was a composite of all Laurie's sharpest memories: 'wine smells of noon and sweet wood smoke of evening, the strings of mules crawling through huge brown landscapes, the wood ploughs scratching the dusty fields . . . the silences of the Sierras, the cracking of sun-burnt rocks . . . bloodstained bull rings, weeping Virgins and tortured Christs . . . all this lay anchored between the great troughs of its mountains'.

It is significant that he wrote more about Spain (and some would say better) than about any other region, not excepting his native Gloucestershire. Spain inspired two books and many poems and articles. He carried 'the great square weight of Spain' with him in his mind's eye, undimmed, for fifty years.

In 1950 the lure of southern Spain drew him back again: 'South is where I most wish to be. South are the cornlands wealed with red poppy, the shipwrecked castles, drunken storks in the vineyards . . . farther south lies the land of promise, gold Andalusia.' It was there he felt most at home, having arrived as a wandering tramp long before, sleeping each night 'among the wine-filled fields' and playing a violin in the cafés by day.

He spelled out the special character of Andalusia: the cult of the bull imported from Bronze Age Crete; that of the horseman developed around Seville – ancestor of the Mexican-American cowboy; the wild flamenco gypsy dance and the sad music of the guitar. Andalusia to Laurie was much more than a tourist's dream. An article for the magazine *Mademoiselle* ('Spain, the Gold Syllable') pictured a land of 'starving fishermen and beggar poets, of smugglers, clowns and madmen', its art rooted in prehistory, its farming sprung from the time of Homer. His advice to those who wished to know Andalusia was to travel on small local buses, to learn a little Spanish, to get involved in local events and to wait for things to happen. Then 'the human encounter which is Spain will follow'.

In the years leading up to 1951 Laurie's major preoccupation was the Festival of Britain. This was an echo of the Great Exhibition of 1851, devised to celebrate Britain's post-war recovery and to present her contemporary image to the world. Although junketings of all kinds, from building village bus shelters to historic pageants, took place all over the country, the main focus was London. Here the chief project was a tourist-oriented development on the south bank of the Thames near Waterloo Station, laid waste by the war. Some visitors applauded the more fantastic aspects of the scheme, although others attacked it for its mundaneness. The South Bank Centre, as it became known, attracted as much criticism as praise, especially for the drab uniformity of its architecture. But visitors in their millions flocked to see it.

As a former staff member of the Ministry of Information Laurie was appointed the festival's Curator of Eccentricities and Caption-Writer-in-Chief – surely one of the most unorthodox government job descriptions ever invented. He was a Higher Executive Officer (a Civil Service ranking) at an annual salary rising from £715 to £865.

The post was to last for three years (planning had started in 1948). It entailed collecting inventors' oddities for an exhibit called Eccentrics' Corner and devising captions for some of the fantasy features under construction on the South Bank. Laurie looked to be an ideal incumbent, with his taste for jokes and his writing skills: 'Don't tease the locomotives – penalty forty shillings' or 'Storks nesting over the Birdcage Restaurant'.

A copy of *Punch* magazine from 30 April 1951 satirized the Festival of Britain in then-and-now cartoons. One showed a village that might almost be Slad, contrasting bucolic rural life in 1851 with orderly existence in 1951. A messy, cheerful farmyard had become the clinically tidy site for a library, with a neat and docile bus queue next door. The satire would have appealed to Laurie.

Mildly teasing humour was his forte. He revelled in the Emmet railway in Battersea Pleasure Gardens (an adjunct of the festival site), carrying children between Far Tottering Station and Oyster Creek. These whimsies were based on sketches by the *Punch* cartoonist Emmet, who also invented the White Knight wire figure to stand in the Lion and Unicorn Pavilion, a setpiece on the South Bank. Lewis Carroll's White Knight epitomized the imagination of all great British eccentrics. The pavilion was planned to illustrate 'the paradoxical qualities that go to make up the Briton'.

The eminent architect Misha Black recalled that trying to tell the story of Britain in the pavilion, in a continuous narrative, was like cramming a gallon of exhibits into a pint pot of buildings. He doubted whether visitors took in more than a fraction of what was displayed. He noted that tens of thousands of words by Laurie, the official caption writer, and Lionel Birch, the caption editor, went into the explanatory script. The words were carefully and often brilliantly written, yet 'only a fraction of this verbosity was read'.

An official festival photo shows Laurie looking rather serious, wearing a check jacket, smoking a pipe and leaning against a table cluttered with oddities. A typed caption on the back reads: 'Laurie Lee, the Festival Caption-Writer, with some of the eccentricities (smoke-grinding machine, egg roundabout, etc.) he has been collecting for exhibition in the Eccentrics' Corner of the South Bank Exhibition, 12 April 1951.'

In 1976 a record of the festival, *A Tonic to the Nation*, appeared in book form. In it Charles Plouviez, who had worked in the festival office, contributed a delightful pen-portrait of his colleague Laurie, who had been 'swept' into the Eccentrics' Corner of the Lion and Unicorn Pavilion when his captions were finished. 'His office up the corridor had become a small museum of oddities, and he was forever showing off his latest finds. He sauntered into my office one day with a violin and mandolin made from matchsticks, and . . . gave a spirited performance of a Telemann concerto.'[3]

A London art critic, G.S. Whittet, also remembered Laurie at the Festival of Britain Press Office: 'a jolly interlude when the small room rang to the twanging guitar and rubicund voice of Laurie Lee in what seems at this distance to have been a rumty-tumty Gloucestershire calypso. Maybe *Cider with Rosie* would have made a good musical. It struck a note of the spirit of gaiety that pervaded everything.'

Another leading poet, Roy Fuller, observed with surprise how many of his friends had festival jobs – among them Laurie, whose 'fantastic cast of mind was translated into curious actualities in the Lion and Unicorn feature'.

Christopher Barry, son of the festival's Director General, Gerald Barry, recalled touring the South Bank site with his father, previously editor of the *News Chronicle*. 'My recollections begin with a visit to the construction site. I particularly recall entering the shadowy half-finished Dome of Discovery and our feeling of excitement as we mounted the concrete ramp. Laurie was Chief Caption Writer under Lionel Birch, and I know how important my father – as a newspaper editor – regarded good captions to be. He very much enjoyed Laurie's Eccentricities exhibit.'[4]

Crowds flocked to festival events in London, and every town and village rose to the occasion with some event to mark 1951 as a renewal year in national history. Laurie's own county of Gloucestershire had a festival village singled out to represent new rural housing. This was Stanton, near Broadway, commended to tourists for a row of council houses built in honey-yellow Cotswold stone. Other Cotswold villages planted a tree or put up a seat on the village green. The novelist John Moore made Bredon, not far from Slad, the setting for *Dance and Sky-lark*, a light-hearted skit on festival-mania.

For six months the country celebrated. A converted aircraft carrier, the *Campania*, carried a floating festival round the ports of Britain. A fleet of a hundred lorries transported a similar land-based carnival. In April the festival had sprung to life with a grand service at St Paul's Cathedral, and in September it ended with fireworks and brass bands on the South Bank.

When it was all over the South Bank fixtures and fittings were sold off at a public auction. There was a scramble for souvenirs. The event was reviewed with mixed emotions as a semi-successful display of pride and fun after the grim wartime and austere post-war years. Honours were handed out to those who had helped to put it all together. Knighthoods went to Gerald Barry and to Hugh Casson, the Chief Architect. Four people were created Companions of the British Empire, eight were awarded Orders of the British Empire, and ten were made Members of the British Empire. Among the ten was listed 'L.E.A. Lee, Exhibitions Department'.

The boy from Gloucestershire was now Laurie Lee, MBE, with a place in the ranks of the establishment, and he went to Buckingham Palace to be presented with his medal by King George VI.

After the festival there was a lull when he travelled a good deal – to Mexico, Trinidad, Barbados, Jamaica, the South of France and elsewhere – which provided inspiration for future writings; he also planned his next two books and wrote more poetry. His third collection of poems, *My Many-Coated Man*, came out in 1955. Many of its poems were love poems, for Laurie was in love with Kathy – and with life.

The title of the new collection, taken from the last verse of an oft-quoted poem, dealt with the ambivalence at the heart of nature – its beauty, its violence: 'Like these, my many-coated man/shields his hot hunger from the wind/and, hooded by a smile, commits/his private murder in the mind.' The poem's title provided a theme for Laurie's memorial service forty years later, and the poem characterized all that was best in his verse. He created unforgettable images in the mind; and always in the background the listener was aware of that particular landscape and life which Laurie carried with him from childhood on. The rank red fox, the stoat, the mottled moth camouflaged against a blotched tree-bark: these belonged to Gloucestershire beechwoods.

Love poems from all his work are among the best remembered of Laurie Lee's verses. 'First Love' equated the desired girl with young life in the natural world, with eggs and glow worms and wild crocuses. 'Summer Rain' brought together life and death, and summer was personified in sorrow. The most purely sensuous of the love poems was surely 'Day of These Days':

> Such a morning it is when love
> leans through the geranium windows
> and calls with a cockerel's tongue . . .
> . . . the cheeks of girls

are as baked bread to the mouth
As bread and beanflowers
the touch of their lips.

Here were echoes of Shakespeare's lovers, Lorenzo and Jessica, in *The Merchant of Venice* and perhaps of Thomas Mendip and Jennet Jourdemayne in Christopher Fry's play *The Lady's Not for Burning*.

If the collection *My Many-Coated Man* had a theme it was that things were often not what they seemed. In human life as in nature there was camouflage, innocent deception and paradox. 'Sunken Evening' identified London's Trafalgar Square with an underwater world, the currents of city movement with fish – lobster-buses, an oyster-pot, prawn-blue pigeons. In 'Apples' the fruits were worlds to be devoured or savoured. The enticing colours might disguise sourness or decay ('the bent worm enters in'), but the poet accepted whatever came his way.

The concept of opposites was strong in 'Scot in the Desert', where the blue-eyed northerner alone could withstand the terrible heat and agony of the desert. As with 'Apples', 'Bombay Arrival' highlighted the rottenness that could lie at the core of outward charm. The islands were cows, the sailing dhow a moth, the port was 'screened with silk'. But, under this, Bombay was 'false as a map . . . a crumbling mask with bullet pores'. That attraction was only skin-deep, a cloak for violence, was also the message of 'My Many-Coated Man'. The tiger, the fox and the moth were linked to killing and disease. More obscure was the vision of the many-coated man who 'commits his private murder in the mind'. Perhaps Laurie sought to conjure up an image of man the primeval hunter.

The highlight of this verse collection was 'The Edge of Day' (also the title given to the American edition of *Cider with Rosie*), which offered a brilliant evocation of daybreak that related dawn to fire (smoky smuts, hot sparks, burning clinkers, molten worlds). The sun rose phoenix-like from ashes and exploded into life. The contrasts that characterized all these poems come together vividly in 'The Edge of Day'; nothing on the surface was the same as at its heart.

The imagery in this book of verse was drawn almost entirely from the natural world. Some of it was quite conventional ('neat as an egg', the 'birdlike stars', the 'mottled moth', the 'frenzied beetle', the 'bounce of rabbits'); but his personification often surprised – the 'waltzing wasp', the pale domestic kiss of Kent', the 'dawn's precise pronouncement' and, most memorably, 'The slow night trawls his heavy net/And hauls the clerk to Surbiton.'

Bombay, Surbiton, Kent; not all Laurie's settings were Cotswold-based, but in most of these poems the poet's mental landscape was recognizably the world he grew up in, and the sounds (as in 'The Abandoned Shade') were the sounds he heard as a boy. Home was where his heart was: 'My heart's keel slides to rest among the meadows.'

In 1956 he was elected a Fellow of the Royal Society of Literature. The Fellowship brought new rewards: at a meeting in the December after he was elected he gave a reading of his own poetry, together with the novelist L.A.G. Strong, another old friend. However, his status was short-lived, for he resigned from the Royal Society in March 1959 in a letter to the Secretary, saying: 'I'm very strongly under the impression that I wrote to you just before Christmas saying that I was forced to cut down on subscriptions and would regretfully have to resign my Fellowship. (Or did I mention it to you at Lady Hamilton's party?) I know you were sympathetic.' There is little doubt that he was in financial difficulties at the time, and it is ironic that this letter was written just six months before the publication of *Cider with Rosie*, which was to alter his life and his finances so radically.

P.J. (Patrick) Kavanagh, a distinguished poet nearly twenty years younger than Laurie, knew him well during the 1950s. In 1956 Patrick Kavanagh married Rosamond Lehmann's daughter Sally, who died tragically young two years later. He still rates Laurie's poems highly, and he included 'Invasion Summer' in his *Oxford Book of Short Poems*. He has paid tribute to Laurie's poetry on more than one occasion, reading from 'Field of Autumn', 'Pollard Beech' and 'April Rise'. He attributed to Laurie's poems 'a Spanish luxuriance of vocabulary and metaphor. I have always felt he was influenced by Spanish poetry, especially Lorca – a sensuousness, a delight, and also some deep regret as at a road not taken, some split in himself, which gives his poetry at its best a religious note, a universality.'[5]

Laurie and Patrick Kavanagh belonged to a widespread arts community that centred on the Fulham Road in west London. Here artists, journalists, actors and poets met in pubs and cafés, promoted their work and spent convivial evenings. Gill Chambers remembered the Fulham Road crowd from her time as a student and part-time waitress from the mid-1950s on. 'I used to work in a café called the Hot Pots opposite the Queen's Elm pub where they all met. In those days pubs didn't do food, so my job was to go across and call them when the café food was ready. I think the Hot Pots lived off sobering up people from the Queen's Elm.'

She was an illustrator and librarian, studying at that time at the Central School of Art. Among the Fulham Road regulars she recalled over the years she mentioned the actor Hugh Burden, (Admiral) Caspar John (son of Augustus John) and Julie Christie. 'I knew enough about Laurie Lee as a poet to feel wide-eyed when I saw him. He was often in the Queen's Elm, and later, when my children read *Cider with Rosie* at school, I was proud to tell them I'd met the author.'

Patrick Kavanagh has entertaining memories of Laurie the social animal: 'He has been called flirtatious, and he was, with both men and women, but in a special way. He took time and used patience, not only to make people feel warm towards him, but also warm towards themselves. He was a prankster and in the traditional sense a gamester. He once told me that he was thrown out of a darts competition [eight and a half feet from throwing point to board] for entering it with an eight-foot blowpipe. Typical.'

Over the years the two poets met often, and latterly Patrick Kavanagh lived in the Cotswolds, ten or twelve miles from Slad. Their forty-year friendship endured, so that he would look back and say publicly: 'I first met Laurie in my twenties, I think at a pub in the Fulham Road. He was a poet I very much admired. He took me aside and said "We poets" – he was including me in that magical brotherhood – "we poets never quite read the poem we want to read, so we have to go away and write it ourselves." I never heard anyone describe a poet's calling better than that. He was extremely well read. The last time I saw him he was quoting reams of a little-known poem by Wordsworth.'

As well as the Fulham Road crowd there was the Soho crowd, centred on the Colony Room and the French House. These places in the 1950s were to London a little of what Montparnasse was to Paris in the 1890s, the stamping ground of a multinational circle of hard-drinking artists, writers and theatre people. What a modern art critic called its 'regulars and irregulars' included Francis Bacon and Lucien Freud, Brendan Behan and Daniel Farson.

Laurie, the near-penniless and struggling poet, even with two books of verse and two plays to his credit, drank with famous names of the 1950s, and in Soho he encountered the Post-Impressionist painter Matthew Smith, the only person to inspire by name one of Laurie's poems. 'To Matthew Smith' celebrated the artist's exuberant colours ('oil is incendiary on your moving brush'), his brilliant landscapes ('your hands are jets that crack the landscape's clinker') and his vivid nude flesh tones ('These molten moments brazed in field and flesh').

Gradually Laurie's circle of acquaintance widened, as he and Kathy began to be asked to publishers' parties and events connected with the Arts Council, the British Council and the Society of Authors. Post-war literary London was an exhilarating place to live.

One of his poems often quoted by fellow poets for its conciseness, wit and mastery of language is 'Pollard Beech'. In each of its eight lines the poet likened the necessary lopping of the beech tree to an aspect of linguistic blue-pencilling which 'edits the sprawled loquacious beech/And clips each hyperbolic leaf'. This perfectly reflected what Patrick Kavanagh called the rhythm and logic behind his sometimes curious images.

'Stork in Jerez' and 'Pollard Beech' were less typical of Laurie's poems in their structure and rhyme. An interview broadcast in the 1990s shed light on Laurie's attitude to language: 'I grew up close to the Bible and Shakespeare, and the oral tradition of the villagers. They spoke naturally; perhaps their vocabulary was not wide, but they were masters of what that vocabulary was capable of communicating. They didn't talk about level playing fields . . . I knew the King James Bible and its sounds, but they were swept away by the modern Bible. How impoverished we all are these Sundays. Where the old Bible says "Arise, take up they bed and walk", the modern version says "Get up and go home," sounding like a policeman. That's one of my favourite grouses, how language has become impoverished and the young are strangled by the second rate.' [6]

In 1957 Laurie wrote the commentary for *Journey Into Spring*, a modest half-hour nature film made for British Transport Films. The film was ground-breaking in its day, showing wildlife in close-up in Gilbert White's Hampshire village of Selborne. Shots of birds nesting, fledgelings hatching out and fish spawning were not commonplace then as they are today. *Journey Into Spring* won many awards. Laurie's commentary, read by the actor Stephen Murray, was both poetic and observant: 'This is England, hanging on the lip of spring'; 'Rooks are community birds who will argue about anything'; 'the wild cherry, burdened with bees and blossom'; 'The skylark rises, a dot of singing darkness.' *Journey Into Spring* was the second collaboration between Laurie and the director Ralph Keene, who had been his cameraman and companion in Cyprus.

In 1958 Laurie contributed an introduction to an art book entitled *A Camera Study of the Artist at Work*. This was a photographic collection based around the sculptures of Jacob Epstein. The writer and sculptor moved in the same artistic circles, which included Augustus John, Elisabeth Frink and several eminent portrait painters and illustrators, among them John Ward who would later do line drawings for Laurie's best-known writing. He stood poised on the verge of international literary triumph, with four books behind him, a dozen film scripts, festival and radio plays, an MBE and a following among poetry lovers.

13

The Rosie Years

That was her beginning, an apparition
of rose in the unbreathed airs of his love,
her heart revealed by the wash of summer.

– 'First Love'

THROUGH the second half of the 1950s Laurie Lee was working on
the first part of his autobiography. He said that it took him nearly
four years, working with difficulty 'in Chelsea garrets'. A major moti-
vation at this stage was his increasing disillusion with London life, a
yearning to rediscover his roots. Part of the revision was done on holiday in Ibiza: he joked that the sea mist compelled him to iron his note-
books. 'I'd come to Ibiza to finish a book, because I write on wine, and
it's cheaper.'[1]

Years later, in the *New York Times Book Review*, he described the
pains and pleasures of telling one's life story. He was impelled, he
wrote, by the fear that a whole decade might drift away and leave
'nothing but a salt-caked mud-flat'. Another urge to write, he suggested, might be to leave messages for those who came after; but his
chief driving force was a desire to celebrate the life he had had and so
preserve it for ever.

As it happened, the end of his childhood had coincided with the
later stages of an almost feudal way of life in the Cotswolds 'until war
and the motor car put an end to it'. Looking back from middle age he
saw Slad in the 1920s as another country. Having to retrace his early
steps was like following a maze and needing to compress a forest into a
single tree.[2]

The difficulties of selection increased with age. Laying out the
rooms of one's past is one thing, he found, but choosing the indispens-
able furniture another. In a passage often quoted as evidence of

Laurie's embroidery of facts, he wrote: 'In another chapter I describe a day that never happened', and he proposed that perhaps a thousand days yielded a single moment, each moment individually true but not in fact sequential. 'The only truth is what you remember. No one else who was there can agree with you because he has his own version of what he saw.' This seems as good a justification as any for autobiographical licence – a journalist called it Laurie's specialism, the 'slippery path between myth and memoir'.[3]

Although the world of his childhood had been a small, parochial one, its details loomed massively to him as a boy. In retrospect, he saw a huge landscape clouded by the years and 'thickly matted by rumour and legend'. He hinted, and others confirmed, that rumour and legend played a large part in those memories. Some critics have claimed that the dividing line between myth and reality cannot clearly be made out. But as Laurie himself put it, 'There is no pure truth, only the moody accounts of witnesses.'[4]

Cider with Rosie was published by the Hogarth Press in November 1959. Within a month it was reprinted three times. Cynics have said that his stock in trade was a lost rural world and that he was promoted as part of a nostalgia industry, but evidently the book touched a chord in its readers. Forty years after its first publication it has sold more than six million copies worldwide

It won instant acclaim from book reviewers. Harold Nicolson, chief literary critic of the *Observer*, referred to its 'rapturous beauty'. C.V. Wedgwood, the historian, wrote of his poet's assurance and originality and his artist's eye: 'His writing, prose or poetry, glows and flames with colour.' The novelist H.E. Bates said that his prose 'flashed and winked like a prism'.

The local Stroud newspaper, the *Stroud News*, did not immediately review the book; after all, it was more than twenty years since Laurie had lived in the area, and he was not particularly well known as an author. However, the paper's gossip columnist, named only as Jonathan, heralded its publication on 13 November 1959. 'Behind the somewhat fatuous title, *Cider with Rosie*, Laurie Lee has written a remarkable book . . . it very definitely establishes Mr Lee as Stroud's own poet and writer.' The columnist was impressed by Laurie's incisive and poetic writing style. 'Full of wise saws and modern instances though the book is, I do not feel that Mr Lee was writing just to catch the eye of the public. If he had had that intention originally, it was submerged by the onrush of memory.' Jonathan noted that Laurie 'did not bend over' to give the book a local setting, yet 'the simple annals of the poor Lee family – for they were certainly poor in the material sense but immensely rich in the things of the spirit – take on the quality of high adventure'.[5]

The journalist declared an interest in having had a childhood not unlike Laurie's: his mother, too, was in domestic service, and he recalled village life in the 1920s. He quoted admiringly from 'Winter and Summer', the passage on the boy carol singers struggling through the snow under the stars to a realization of what the first Christmas had been like. And, perceptively, he compared *Cider with Rosie* to Richard Jeffries's *Bevis*, a portrait of country life written by a Wiltshire farmer's son in 1882. He detected similarities between the two, sixty years apart in time but less than sixty miles in distance.

No readers immediately responded to the Stroud review, but the newspaper followed up its story by telephoning Laurie in London. 'Mr Lee told the *News* that *Cider with Rosie* had sold 18,000 copies in three weeks, and he had given a reading at Foyle's Bookshop in London with Peggy Ashcroft, who read some of his poems.' Jonathan was pleased to note that London reviewers endorsed his praise for the book, but he was displeased at their inaccuracies – in particular a tendency to report that Laurie had been born in Slad. This was seen as an affront to Stroud.

The *Daily Telegraph* critic Margaret Lane also praised *Cider with Rosie*. She commented that writing about one's childhood could be a snare. If the childhood years were happy it was virtually impossible to transmit that 'golden haze'. Laurie, she said, took the reader 'straight into humble hedgerow, cottage and village' but without falling into sentimentality. She perceived warmth and affection, 'cheerful squalor and church outings' and a world far removed from 'the heresy that country childhood and poverty are all paradise'. She drew an analogy with Flora Thompson's *Lark Rise to Candleford*, published in 1939, in terms of its loving dwelling on domestic detail and its poet's eye.[6]

Inevitably there were complaints. *Cider with Rosie* was not a factual account of the past. It was a poet's vision of his youth, created after a gap of thirty-five years. Not everyone from that past was entirely happy with Laurie's version of his childhood. He dedicated the book to his brothers and sisters, 'the half and the whole'. Certain relatives took exception to the profiles of two of the Light brothers, Ray and Sid, whose weaknesses were thought to be uncharitably exaggerated; and a few local people dismissed the book as a pack of lies.

However, great excitement was generated in the Stroud area, still a quiet country district, especially among villagers who achieved instant fame. Laurie's cousin, Charlie Light, recalled that his sister Edith was working at the Imperial Hotel in Stroud when the book came out. 'People she didn't know kept coming in and saying they were mentioned in the book.' Many of them claimed relatives, connections and recollections. Some wished that their families had not been so vividly spotlighted.

There was also the controversy over the piano factory. In the first edition Laurie had written: 'There was a fire at the piano factory almost every year. It seemed to be a way of balancing the books . . . one heard thundering chords as the pianos started crashing about.' In 1911 Bentley's Piano Works, a highly reputable company, had moved from north London to an empty cloth mill at Woodchester. There it was renamed the Stroud Piano Company, where it still flourishes as the Woodchester Piano Company. The only major fire at the mill occurred in 1938, some fifteen years after the period Laurie was supposedly writing about. The owners sued for libel, and Laurie and his publishers settled out of court for a sum rumoured to be in the region of £30,000. The local press did not report the event.

In the second edition, a few months later, the story was changed to: 'There was a fire at the boiler works almost every year . . . when we got there we found it a particularly good one . . . ceilings and floors fell in, windows melted like icicles . . . we used up a lot of the day cheering each toppling chimney.' The piano factory affair was a local talking point for years.

Contemporaries from the 1920s have differing memories of childhood in Slad – as Laurie freely acknowledged. Jim Fern, in his book
Ferns in the Valley, remembered Annie's cottage as a treasure chest of
china knick-knacks where he was invited in to eat bread and dripping.
Some of Laurie's younger cousins more realistically compared it to a
jumble sale.[7] Jim Fern remembered Laurie as an older boy whom he
looked up to; but at the age of eleven Laurie went to the Central Boys'
School, he a few years later to the grammar school. After that their
paths seldom crossed, and when Laurie returned to live in Slad Jim
Fern was living elsewhere. What is real and recognizable, and uni-
formly recollected by their generation, was the tight-knit community
of boys who played together, sang in the choir and went on outings
from the grey-stone village in the Cotswold valley. Laurie carried that
image with him always, and it never faded.

Some of the incidents described hover nearer to myth than history.
Older residents have only vague memories of Miss Flynn's suicide –
she was Miss Fluck in early editions – or the man who was killed at the
crossroads (opinion divides on where he came from, whether he was
murdered for his gold watch or simply in a drunken brawl or whether
he was murdered at all). Even more doubt attaches to the ghostly
stagecoach at Bulls Cross. But are not these legitimate schoolboy tales?

The frail and aged Joe and Hannah Brown, however, are well
remembered, as was the shock in Slad when they were removed to the
Stroud Workhouse. So were the two Grannies who lived under the
same roof as the Lees and Squire Jones at Steanbridge House, whose
name crops up often in official records. More than one contemporary
spoke of Mr Jones's funeral in 1925.

Reminiscing in the 1990s, Laurie said: 'My old schoolmate Jim
brings parties up from Stroud to look round the village. I try not to get
involved. A few of my schoolfellows still live hereabouts – Betty
Gleed, the Robinsons; Eileen Brown, who used to play the piano while
I fiddled, she died three years ago.' (Betty Gleed became Mrs Spring
and lived in Stroud.) And he added: 'I sometimes walk past Lee's Cottage – it's now called Rosebank. It's known locally as Laurie Lee's
Cottage, although I haven't been inside it for sixty years.' He liked to

say that the present owners had been 'pestered by pilgrims' who stared in at the windows and invaded the garden to take snaps. And he claimed that a man up the road said that if he had known earlier what he now knew he would have bought the place and opened it up for cream teas.[8]

To anyone who asked him about Rosie, Laurie would only say with a mysterious – and mischievous – smile: 'She was someone, she was anyone, she was no one.' Names of girls crop up in the book like flowers. When he was twelve there was Jo, with her 'speechless grace' – his very first bite at the apple. There was Poppy Green, aged five, 'like a portable sweet shop'. There was Lizzie with 'large bottle blue eyes', but she was deeply religious and lashed out with a bag of crayons at the first boy who intercepted her in the wood.

As Laurie grew up in the village, so his interests had focused on two girls. 'Bet was brazen and Rosie was provocative.' Betty, he asserted, would have stripped in church for a wine gum. Rosie led him a dance round the barns and fowlhouses. And so to the hayfield. Was she Rosie Burdock, as he named her in the book, or Rosie Green or Rosie Harris? Various local women have been nominated for the honour of being the eponymous heroine of the autobiography. But he never told, and the claimants can do no more than say: 'I lived in Slad and I knew Laurie.' There were no witnesses, and old friends can only speculate – and there are no Burdocks currently living in the Stroud area. A Cheltenham resident whose maiden name was Rosalind Green had as good a claim as any to the title; she regretted having to buy her own copy of the book. Members of the family believe that Rosie was not one but many girls.

Towards the end of Cider with Rosie Laurie sketched in the later careers of some of the protagonists. Jo, he said, married a Painswick baker, Bet went to Australia and Rosie married a soldier. We can safely assume that Laurie knew more than one girl called Rosie, that there was cider in the fields at haymaking time, that he probably did make love under a haywagon. The rest is speculation – or a secret.

In 1983 an illustrated Cider with Rosie was published, full of sepia photographs of the Lee family and old views of the Slad Valley. Many readers have assumed that the idyllic portrait of a flaxen-haired 'Rosie' in a straw hat, carrying a basket of flowers, was the true Rosie, even though no place or date was given. The exceptional quality of the picture suggests to some that it was taken by Laurie himself, as he was later to develop into a talented photographer; 'Rosie', however, was not credited with a surname. Another piece of evidence, often cited, was a school photograph taken about 1920 which named Laurie, Jack and Rosie in the caption but did not identify who was who. Towards the end of the book Rosie was described as hefty, with sly cat-like eyes and a curling mouth – not the image most readers conjure up of Laurie's first love. Journalists, film agents and theatre producers have struggled in vain to track down the real Rosie, and indeed in a musical and visual tribute to the author, staged in Stroud after his death, six local 'Rosies' of Laurie's generation were present in the audience.

The greatest material change brought to Laurie and Kathy's life by the publication of *Cider with Rosie* was that it financed the buying of a small house in Slad, little more than a stone's throw from Lee's Cottage. It is a moot point whether Laurie always intended to return there or whether the Stroud estate agents pointed him in that direction.

At one time the eighteenth-century house, little changed since it was first built, had belonged to Jim Fern's grandfather. It stands just below the Woolpack Inn, giving uninterrupted views across the Slad Valley to the farms where Laurie played as a boy. A step up from his new home was the inn, a step up from there the church where he used to sing in the choir. Slad had changed surprisingly little, but Laurie's relationship with it had changed immeasurably.

The Lees kept on their Chelsea flat – where Laurie did most of his writing – but moved to Slad in the autumn of 1962 and spent their days happily settling into Rose Cottage with its 'long raftered attic, heavy doors, Victorian range, outdoor tap and lavatory'. Later they moved next door to Little Court. They cut firewood, created a garden and painted the house. Some of Laurie's old neighbours were, he said, quite fidgety at seeing the author of *Cider with Rosie* again – but 'I'd brought her [Kathy] back to my beginnings, a re-starting and starting ground for us both'.

He rewrote *Cider with Rosie* three times, gave it to the publishers and assumed that he would hear no more. A printers' strike, he later said, propelled *Cider with Rosie* to the top of the booksellers' charts. The book, intended to come out in the summer ('so brilliant with sun that no one could read except down a coal hole'), was delayed till Christmas present-buying time, when few new books were around: 'Rosie began selling like hot-pokered cider . . . under Christmas trees all over the country it was exchanged like a ritual.'

A year after it was published *Cider with Rosie* was serialized in the London *Evening Standard* and won the W.H. Smith Literary Award. The actress Peggy Ashcroft presented the £1,000 cheque for the award to Laurie at the Savoy Hotel. For a struggling author £1,000 was a lot of money, and royalties now came pouring in.

He wrote an article for the *Evening Standard* about his new status. 'Few poets, save the dead, make a living today,' he wrote. 'I have been forced to chop sticks when I would rather have been planting trees.' A writer could always make money by writing 'candy floss pop songs, telly jingles, or ghost books for generals'. But to be given an advance by his publishers and told to write what he liked had been his great incentive.[9]

Then came something of a backlash, when Stroud people began reading the book. 'It's difficult to say who were the most enraged – those who recognized themselves, or who thought they did, or those who found they had been left out.' Laurie admitted that the reactions shook him ('a chill wind blew from the west'), but when he started apologizing and offering to cut offended people from the next edition they were equally offended. He spent much of the ensuing summer opening fêtes – 'far from being the squat-nosed scab-skinned urchin they remembered, I was briefly the valley's favourite son'.

Finding that he had produced a best-seller was, he said, a mixture of grit and honey. 'Some friends avoid you, and total strangers invite you, letters arrive demanding advice, and people get your name right at last.' Seeking to analyse the book's popularity, he attributed it partly to a form of reader-envy. 'Perhaps the mud and poverty among which we lived, the naked seasons that surrounded us, our home-made fires and satisfactions . . . have provided for the more affluent reader . . . a reminder of roots not so long cut off, a kind of envy for a raw life gone.'

Whatever the causes, it soon became obvious that he was the high priest of a boyhood nostalgia cult among writers. *Cider with Rosie* as a *roman-à-clef* was compared with Alain-Fournier, James Joyce and Rudyard Kipling. Others followed where Laurie Lee led. His poems were reprinted, he gave public readings, he was anthologized.

One of the first and best selections of Lee verse alongside other poets in an anthology was in *Poets of Our Time*, edited in 1965 by F.E.S. Finn. The poets selected included John Betjeman, Charles Causley, Ted Hughes, Norman Nicholson and R.S. Thomas. The editor chose fifteen of Laurie Lee's poems and commented in his introduction to them: 'His use of imagery is reminiscent of the Metaphysical poets.' Referring to Laurie's intensity he quoted from 'Bombay Arrival' and 'Field of Autumn'; 'Home from Abroad' and 'April Rise' are also singled out. This anthology brings together work by Laurie and several of his friends: Charles Causley, Patric Dickinson and Alan Ross. 'Home from Abroad' was later selected for inclusion in Kevin Crossley-Holland's *Oxford Book of Travel Poems*.

Within a few years *Cider with Rosie* had sold a million copies; by 1994 five times that number; by 1997, the year of his death, six million. It is impossible to calculate how many schoolchildren around the world have read it as a set text for English literature examinations; and a fair number have studied his poems for English literature A-levels. Not many books about a rural childhood ('like a tale told in a pub', he once said) have had this kind of exposure and yet generated so much pleasure.

The 1950s were also a career high point for Laurie's brother Jack. He directed three of his most successful films – *A Town Like Alice* (1956), *Robbery Under Arms* (1957) and *The Captain's Table* (1959).

Soon after this he settled permanently in Australia, returning at regular intervals to visit his relatives, among them Laurie. He was at his brother's funeral in 1997, looking, at eighty-four, remarkably fit and youthful: the last survivor of Reg and Annie Lee's talented family.

14

The Golden Years

... lying with my orchid love,
whose kiss no frost of age can sever,
I cannot doubt the cold is dead,
The gold earth turned to good – forever.
                              – 'Scot in the Desert'

BACK in his familiar valley, happily married, an established author at the peak of his writing powers, Laurie had one unfulfilled ambition: to have a child with Kathy. And in 1963 this was achieved.

He and Kathy had been together more than twelve years, by then half fearing that she would never conceive. Laurie attributed Jessy's conception when he was approaching fifty to the changed and calmer rhythm of their lives away from London. Kathy herself said that it was due to a minor operation.

Laurie hid Mexican corn dollies under the bed that spring and summer as fertility charms and described rousing neighbours one autumn night in October 1963 to drive Kathy the four miles to Stroud Maternity Hospital, then ringing the hospital agitatedly at intervals from the village telephone box. Finally the matron, Laurie's cousin Marion, came on the line: 'That you, Laurie? You got a daughter ... What's the matter with you? Dropped dead or something? You better hurry on round.'[1]

Marion was matron at Stroud Maternity Hospital for more than twenty years, seeing through at least two thousand births. She said that Jessy's birth had been difficult but that she was a fine healthy baby. She has a copy of *Two Women*, inscribed by Laurie: 'Life begins with Marion ... to Cousin Marion, to whom I am deeply indebted for at least half this book – with love and gratitude from Laurie and The Two.'

The family would sit by the cottage fire in the lamplight, Kathy breast-feeding while Laurie played Schubert records. Jessy's birth had bowled him over. 'The Firstborn', an essay published soon after in London's *Evening Standard,* outlines a sense of wonder and achievement, as if he had not deserved such late happiness. It is perhaps significant that she was born in autumn, always for Laurie a particularly poignant and emotional time of year.

She dropped into his life, he wrote, like a bruised plum, 'a blind and protesting dwarf'. Her cry was like a Hebridean lament. She filled the cottage with her personality, and at night he took her to bed and studied her like a book. For Laurie, her life was his second life, and he simply could not believe his luck. He wished for her two gifts: a relish for life, and an awareness of the past, when to be a child brought its own rewards.[2]

The essay was a beautiful prose poem celebrating fatherhood. Having a child, he admitted, changed a man's priorities and altered his whole life. A child was not an ego-extension or a plaything but a responsibility to guard for ever. The piece surprises by its intimacy. Many fathers would have found it embarrassing to share their emotions quite so publicly. Not so Laurie. It had seemed that Kathy would never conceive, and now the miracle had happened and he wanted to tell the world.

He did more than write about Jessy's childhood and adolescence. Over the years he took endless photographs of mother and daughter, with a skill perhaps acquired during his script-writing days. He put them by to be assembled into an album, as portrait artists painted their favourite models again and again.

The five years after Jessy's birth were occupied by writing the delayed second volume of his autobiography. He could hardly put it off any longer after the enormous success of the first book, which, after all, took his life only to the age of nineteen. *Cider with Rosie* had left off with a glimpse of old men in Cotswold pubs singing 'As I Walked Out' while the adolescent Laurie scribbled poems in his bedroom and contemplated his future.

The new book drew its title from the song and added another

image – that of Laurie leaving Slad on foot to see the world on a June morning: not quite twenty, carrying a violin, a tent and some food. *As I Walked Out One Midsummer Morning* may not have sold as well as *Cider with Rosie*, but many critics regard it as his best work.

Looking back thirty-five years to the rites of passage that had propelled him through his busking and labouring years, from Southampton to Bournemouth to London to Vigo to Madrid to Málaga, he may have glossed over the hardships – although not the poverty – and exaggerated the pleasures. But they were also the years that consolidated his personality and guided him into a writing career. The landscapes of the past, the places he passed through in his early twenties, had determined the kind of person he was going to be. From Mother Lee's cottage at Slad to the Hotel Mediterráneo at Almuñécar was one of those journeys, like Don Quixote's or Tristram Shandy's, that made the man.

As I Walked Out One Midsummer Morning was published in 1969 by André Deutsch (who was to be Laurie's publisher for more than a decade) and was dedicated to T. S. Matthews, an Anglo-American journalist and former newspaper editor. It included delicate stippled drawings, chiefly of Spanish scenes, by Leonard Rosoman, best known as a stage designer. Within ten years it was reprinted ten times. The sequel to *Cider with Rosie* could not fail to establish its author even more firmly in the reading public's consciousness, and demand swiftly developed for a third instalment. This was not to appear for more than twenty years.

The second book was every bit as much a *roman-à-clef* as *Cider with Rosie*, narrating Laurie's passage from adolescence into manhood, tracing his growth from Cotswold boy to Spanish warrior. It opened with a glance back at his childhood, his mother waving him goodbye from the bank above Lee's Cottage; and it ended looking ahead provocatively in the Spanish Pyrenees: 'I was back in Spain, with a winter of war before me.'

The years between are probably a fair account of his busking in seaside towns and pushing a builder's barrow in London. There were references to girl-friends who cannot easily be identified after sixty years, but there is no reason to suppose that they did not exist: the 'fluid young girl in a gym slip' whom he cuddled on Bognor Regis beach, Cleo the Anglo-American from Putney Heath (disappointingly, more interested in politics than sex), the sexily confident eight-year-old Patsy Flynn, Nell from Balham who begged him to take her with him to Spain. The building-site workers; the left-wing rabble-rouser who introduced Laurie to strikes and Communism; his various landladies – they all ring true. The reality of those first months away from home was colourful enough to need no glamorizing. The journey across Spain from Vigo to Málaga seems less credible. Could he, in those days before the mass movement of backpackers like lemmings across continents, have travelled almost without money over fifteen hundred miles, with prolonged stops in various Spanish cities, in less than six months? It would be possible today, when car lifts are freely given, but on primitive Spanish roads, where the main transport was horse and cart, in blistering heat, it somewhat strains belief.

He had started to discover Spain. 'My small country school . . . had provided me with nothing more tangible or useful about Spain than that Seville had a barber and Barcelona, nuts.' At first he walked and lived off the land. Then he found that musicians were welcome and that coins were readily given for music such as his. He camped, or slept for next to nothing in village inns, and was given food by music lovers. When he was fit to drop from exhaustion strangers took him by car from Toro to Valladolid; but this is a short distance and one of the only two lifts by motor vehicle that he mentions. (Later two booksellers travelling with missals drove him into Madrid.) A ride on a mule cart into Segovia sounds more convincing. One doubts whether a not over-strong Englishman could have walked over a thousand miles in barely endurable heat through Spain's hottest regions.

The violin-playing is surely believable, as is the story of the policeman who ordered a crowd to put some money in Laurie's hat (although only a single coin materialized) and the encounter with two members of the Guardia Civil who demanded documents but obviously could not read the notes that Laurie hurriedly wrote out himself. In Algeciras he was asked for tunes as varied as *Ave Maria*, airs by Schubert and 'On with the Motley'.

Laurie would have us believe that he resisted most forms of Spanish temptation, which seems surprising in view of his strong interest in English girls. But he succumbed to Concha in a Madrid café and to Consuelito in Valdepeñas, who sought her grandfather's approval first.

In Seville Laurie first viewed the Guadalquivir, and here on the riverbank the play written in 1947 germinated in his mind. 'It was from this narrow river . . . that Columbus sailed to discover America, followed a few years later by the leaking caravelles of Magellan.' The explorers had sailed from some way downriver, nearer to Cádiz, but Laurie gradually familiarized himself with much of the Andalusian coast, so that when he came to write *The Voyage of Magellan* some ten years later he could give Magellan's home port a local habitation and a name. It was in Seville also that a sailor begging a cigarette gave him the first hint of civil war to come.

His encounters with the Chief of Police in Gibraltar and with Karl, a German for whom he wrote English love letters, in Málaga, may have had an element of fantasy; but there was nothing extraordinary about the four drunken British merchant seamen he met near the docks, finding himself landed with the unsavoury task of returning them to their ship.

And so, as he told the story, he arrived in December 1935 in Castillo, as he called the small fishing village of Almuñécar, where he spent some of the happiest months of his life. He could scarcely have guessed that it would one day become a Spanish holiday resort that cushions tourists 'like a sun-warmed lilo', as he was to describe Ibiza in the 1950s. In 1935 Almuñécar had just two hotels. At one of these Laurie was taken on as kitchen help, carpenter and evening musician. He grew to love this place, and it carved itself into the landscape of his mind almost as deeply as Slad. Poems, articles and autobiography testify to his rapport with Andalusia. He was twenty-two, able to understand Spanish, sociable and open to all new impressions.

After the chapter on Castillo the book pitched the reader into a foretaste of the Civil War. In the middle of July café radios went silent and rumour was rife. Franco's troops had landed from Morocco and taken Granada. There was fighting in the streets of Málaga, and a destroyer accidentally shelled Castillo, which was now flying Republican flags.

The town's anxious wait for the advance of Franco's tanks is acutely conveyed. Laurie was writing as a sympathetic observer, a Communist supporter, naturally inclined to side with the Republican Andalusians against the Nationalist rebels. Idealism was part of his character, with perhaps a streak of recklessness. He had felt both excitement and disappointment when a Royal Navy destroyer from Gibraltar moored in the bay to pick up stranded British expatriates. He wrote: 'The King of England had sent a ship for the hotel fiddler.' Who would have guessed that half a century later the resort would put up a statue to that fiddler? This was history, needing no embellishment.

The book covered little more than two years of Laurie's life, but a lifetime of experience had elapsed between the Gloucestershire teenager leaving home with his belongings in a bundle and the return of the traveller, musician, poet and friend of the famous. He had discovered himself and knew where he was going.

In the final chapter of *As I Walked Out One Midsummer Morning* Laurie recalled his brief return to Slad and his restlessness there, followed after a few months by his decision to rejoin his friends in Spain and fight with them against Franco. Then came the passionate farewells to his London lover, who pursued him to Spain in a vain attempt to hold him back, and the arduous winter journey on foot through the Pyrenees.

At last he crossed the border and was able to say in Spanish: 'I've come to join you.' A welcoming '*Pase usted*' was the reply. Impatient readers had to wait twenty-two years for the rest of the story, the account of Laurie's Spanish Civil War. Another product of the Spanish years that came to light in 1969 was the poem 'The Gypsies of Granada' ('Gitano y Gitanas'), written for a collection of verse and drawings celebrating Andalusia. The collection was edited by the artist Jo Jones, superbly produced in a handsome limited edition and dedicated to the memory of the flamenco dancer Carmen Amaya.

A cockerel was yet again the poet's central symbol:

Quick, jungly, dark,
he, the prize bantam,
stepping black-combed
from his hiding shadow,
Gives his split-beak cry,
sets the guitar-gut throbbing
like nerves
stretched across a bone.
Tallied and spurred,
Ready for love or money,
Cocky he straddles
the bushed gorge of the barrio.
. . . Suddenly they come,
clicking their ebony fingers,
spinning their tail feathers
round the jangling fires.[3]

Cockerels, guitars, dancers; together for Laurie they spelled
Andalusia and the heart of Spain.

Later, in 1969, he repaid a debt to Roy Campbell by writing a foreword to his friend's memoir, *Light on a Dark Horse*. It was at Roy
Campbell's house near Marseilles that Laurie first met Kathy, and the
Campbells had befriended him when he was an impoverished Briton
abroad, moneyless and friendless in Toledo. The friendship was a lifelong one until Roy Campbell died in 1957. Laurie summed him up as
'somewhat larger than the life of his day'. He was 'the wounded hunter
bound to his cave . . . whose daggered epigrams could strike instant
death'. He defended his old friend against charges of Fascism (based
on his allegiance to Franco during the Civil War). His poetry, Laurie
said, was a physical engagement with life, a verse parallel to Heming-
way's prose. However profoundly Laurie disagreed with most of his
'dottier prejudices', he had cherished him since their first meeting. The
foreword was a poet's tribute to a fellow poet and the sincere salute of
a friend.[4]

At first glance the two men would seem to have had little but poetry in common: Laurie the itinerant musician and film maker, Roy Campbell the bullfighter, sportsman and flamboyant adventurer. But both were gregarious, loved women passionately, and both fought in the Spanish Civil War, although on opposite sides. The link that chiefly bound Laurie and his friend was surely their love of unsullied open spaces. Roy Campbell grew up in the South African veld. His poems reflected that sunswept landscape as unmistakably as Laurie's poems evoked the windswept Cotswolds.

In the 1960s Laurie counted as friends a number of leading poets. Peter Levi had trained as a Jesuit priest at Heythrop College in Oxfordshire. For ten years he was a lecturer at Campion Hall, Oxford, and in the 1980s was elected Oxford Professor of Poetry. He recalls Laurie being a house guest at Bruern Grange near Heythrop, the country home of Michael Astor. He was one of the Astor clan which included Nancy, the first woman to take her seat in the House of Commons, John Jacob, the American tycoon who died on the *Titanic*, and David, who for twenty-seven years edited the *Observer* newspaper.

Like Cecil Day-Lewis, Peter Levi was a classicist who wrote poetry, detective novels and biography. Much later in his career his path again crossed Laurie's at literature festivals, and he contributed to the theatrical celebration in Cheltenham for Laurie's seventieth birthday. In 1977 he married Deirdre, widow of Cyril Connolly who first published Laurie's poems. The Lee and Levi families lived not twenty miles apart in Gloucestershire in the 1990s. Although the two writers were old friends, Peter Levi was not disinclined to speak his mind in a *Spectator* review of 'talking books' a year after Laurie's death, which included an audio version of *Cider with Rosie,* read by professional actors. 'One of the queerest is an adaptation of that awful liar Laurie Lee, who was my dear friend and whose embroideries of reality have by no means all been discovered yet.' [5]

Another long-standing friend from the 1950s was Alan Ross. He and Laurie lived almost next door to each other in Elm Park Gardens, Chelsea, for thirty years. They were congenial neighbours, visiting local pubs and the Chelsea Arts Club together. Alan Ross recalled Laurie visiting him in Sussex and the two of them staying at the home of Daphne Hardy, otherwise known as the sculptor Daphne Henrion. This was one of a number of contacts Laurie had with sculptors, not least through Kathy's links with Jacob Epstein. Alan Ross summed up his view of Laurie's poetry: 'Lushly romantic, but he is a modern poet, whose choice of words is exact and telling. He is not really like anyone else; his language on the whole sophisticated, not that of a country bumpkin.'

It was both Laurie's good fortune and his misfortune that his poetry-writing period coincided with the heyday of a generation of fine poets who had come to prominence in the 1930s. Charles Causley, Louis MacNeice, W.H. Auden, Elizabeth Jennings, Philip Larkin, Patric Dickinson, Stephen Spender and R.S. Thomas were all writing just after the war. Very different poets John Betjeman and Dylan Thomas belong to the same period; and T.S. Eliot and Robert Graves were still writing. It was a vintage time for British poets.

Works by these poets feature often in anthologies of the post-war decades. The reason for the comparative scarcity of Laurie's work in these may be due in part to his output, amounting to three slim collections, as well as the poems' limitations in terms of form and theme – almost all confined to lyrics dealing with landscapes, wildlife or the seasons – or the fact that he wrote verse only while he was in his thirties. Compared to the prolific output of, say, Cecil Day-Lewis or Ted Hughes, Laurie's poetic *oeuvre* was small.

15
Citizen of the World

For me, alike, this flushed October –
Ripe, and round-fleshed and bellyfull –
Fevers me fast but cannot fright . . .
        – 'Cock Pheasant'

R EFERRING to his rediscovered village life, Laurie explained in a
television interview just before his eightieth birthday: 'We're not
working out a soap opera. We're living our particular history. We know
each other's secrets, but this is part of the life of a community . . . and
I'm part of it. Here I am and here I stay.'[1]

In the 1970s he kept his London flat and retreated there for part of
most weeks. He enjoyed writers' gatherings, the more convivial the
better, and literary festivals. He was comfortably off now and able to
travel abroad when he wished. But from now on Slad was the focal
point of his inspiration, his social life and his family ties. He rented a
room for writing upstairs at the Subscription Rooms, Stroud's Victorian Town Hall. And he gave endless interviews at the Woolpack.

Instead of being Laurie Lee, the poet, he was now to the world
Laurie Lee, the Cotswold author who had written *Cider with Rosie*.
Over the years the book was filmed, serialized, performed by amateur
dramatic societies, broadcast, set as a text for literature examinations
and translated into sixteen languages. Its most-quoted lines developed
a life of their own: 'Never to be forgotten, that first long secret drink
of golden fire, juice of those valleys and of that time, wine of wild
orchards, of russet summer, of plump red apples, and Rosie's burning
cheeks. Never to be forgotten, or ever tasted again.' But the best thing
was to hear Laurie himself read it in his husky Gloucestershire burr.

Having returned to his roots, Laurie drew a new strength from the
fields and wooded valleys of the Cotswolds. His later poems and essays

owe quite as much as his earlier writing to the life of those valleys. Increasingly he became identified with his particular location, so that a critic could say that he embodied 'the semi-peasant spirit of a thousand-year-old tradition'. Laurie was not a historian, but in conversation he often referred to the prehistoric barrows of the Slad Valley and the history of ancient conflict between England and Wales – his home was less than twenty miles from the Welsh border.

By the late 1970s he was consolidating, rewriting and accumulating reprints. The poem 'On Beacon Hill' focused on both local and universal reference points: 'Now as we lie beneath the sky . . ./Visible at last we are/To each nebula and star.' Beacon Hill was a favourite landmark where he often took Jessy for picnics. As she grew up, going first to a London school and then to Cheltenham Ladies' College, Laurie never tired of his daughter's company. She was 'the second force in my life'.

His 1975 collection of essays and articles, *I Can't Stay Long*, repeated his ecstatic original celebration of Jessy in 'The Firstborn'. The book was dedicated 'to Pen and Virginia', an eclectic album of what he calls first loves and obsessions.

Just as the Woolpack was his home from home in Slad, so the Queen's Elm in West London provided a refuge when he was alone in London writing. A handsome 1914 building, it currently lies empty; but for most of Laurie's working life it was a gathering place for a dynamic circle of writers, artists and actors. The pub, an adjoining road and an impressive house take their name from a legend that appealed to Laurie: the story goes that Queen Elizabeth I sheltered here in a downpour and ordered the elm to be named the Queen's Elm. (A less respectable version of the story has her stopping to relieve herself behind the tree.) Records show that an inn stood at the crossroads in 1667, and the decimation of elms this century by Dutch elm disease gives the pub's name a historic distinction.

Laurie calculated that the Queen's Elm was 274 paces from his flat. Here he ate out, escaped from the pressures of meeting deadlines and enjoyed the company of such famous names as the sculptor Elisabeth Frink, the actors Virginia McKenna, Bill Travers and Julie Christie, the cartoonist Jak and the artist Bill Thomson. The Queen's Elm regulars formed a huge larger-than-life family presided over by the genial Irish landlord Sean Treacy, himself an author.

Laurie loved the Queen's Elm fraternity and was moved to write an article about them all. As he said, there were plenty of smarter and more comfortable pubs around. But for him it was 'a relaxed drinking area' where the hawks and the doves of the arts world could meet without friction, attracting the most eclectic bunch of customers to be found under one roof. 'No night's atmosphere is ever the same,' he wrote, 'but . . . blindfold, you would always know you were there.' Laurie attributed it all to the pub's charismatic landlord. Where else, he asked, could you in one evening consult your doctor and bank manager, drink with a television comic, sell some books, be snubbed by a dowager and leave with more money than you entered with?[2]

Jan Treacy, Sean's widow, the theatre and television actress professionally known as Jan Kenny, treasures various mementoes of Laurie: cards sent by him at regular intervals, several signed photographs and a toy mouse with an ridiculously long tail. He kept it in his pocket with the tail hanging out in order to startle people. Jan Treacy spoke of Laurie with warm affection: 'He was our best friend and best man at our wedding in 1977. Afterwards we went to the La Famiglia restaurant in Chelsea, and Laurie sent dozens of red roses to our flat.' They in their turn looked after him whenever he was in London without Kathy. 'We'd make steak and kidney pie or shepherd's pie, something he liked, then he'd take it back to eat while he was working. On the whole he didn't like fancy food, but sometimes he'd go with us to a café in Soho or to the restaurant at the London Zoo.'

She talked movingly of Laurie's last visit to Sean, when her husband lay dying in hospital. 'Laurie said: "Goodbye, old friend", and after the funeral he poured a bottle of whisky over the funeral flowers. It was his way of saying goodbye, their last drink together.'

For some years she ran an art gallery above the Queen's Elm, and the walls of her flat in 1998 are hung with paintings by well-known artists – among them a view of the Lee family cottage at Slad. She treasures, too, a copy of 'Christmas Landscape', the poem written out in Laurie's hand and signed for her, as well as a collection of mostly comic postcards sent by Laurie when he was out of town. One shows two women in hats admiring a sexy statue called 'The Discus Thrower' ('There you are, Gert, the Greeks had a word for it'). Laurie signed this one: 'Yours, The Discus Thrower.' A card to cheer Jan up when she was depressed carries a surreal picture of a man's head. On this Laurie wrote: 'I've been thinking of you; I've been a lot in Gloucestershire cutting back the roses, but I hope to see you soon. Lots of love from your old friend with a hole in his head.'

When he was not at the Queen's Elm Laurie spent much of his leisure at the Chelsea Arts Club, a short walk from his flat, the haunt of artists, writers and show-business people for over a century. It is a low, white early Victorian building which became the Arts Club in 1891. Laurie applied for membership in 1949, after being introduced by Anthony Devas, and in the 1990s he liked to say that he was the oldest member, although an honorary one as a non-artist. He always sat in a corner of the Ladies' Bar and drank Ruddles bitter, an exclusive supply ordered for him by the club. They still have one bottle left. A striking bronze head of Laurie by the sculptor Lyn Bamber now sits in the bar.

The Arts Club garden is an oasis that could be Gloucestershire-in-London, lush and green with innumerable birds and squirrels. The coffee-table centenary book of the club, written by the artist Tom Cross, pays much attention to Laurie and includes two paintings of him. One by Paul Wyeth is called 'Concert at the Chelsea Arts Club 1960'. A cluster of distinguished artists gathers round Laurie, who is dressed in a fur-collared coat and Cossack-style hat and playing a recorder. On the table in front of him is a copy of the recently published *Cider with Rosie*. There is also a portrait by Anthony Devas of Laurie aged about twenty-five, painted when he was lodging at Markham Square.

The centenary book quotes Laurie on the Chelsea Arts Ball, a yearly extravaganza which was said to be the most scandalous event in the social calendar. It was held at the Royal Albert Hall in London until it was banned because of rowdiness. He recalled with glee that 'orgiastic floats used to come swirling round the ballroom covered in girls', some of whom he thought might have been naked.[3]

The club threw an eightieth birthday party for Laurie which is still talked about. Half of literary London attended, and the cake with eighty candles was shaped like a huge violin. And there they held what came to be called 'The Wake', a great reception after the memorial service for him on a bright autumn day in 1997.

Laurie's flat was on an upper floor in a solid Victorian terrace overlooking the leafy plane trees of Elm Park Gardens. This was his London base for more than thirty-five years. Two doors away was the birthplace of the post-war Labour Chancellor of the Exchequer, Sir Stafford Cripps, who in old age made his home in a Cotswold valley not far from Slad. Other haunts of Laurie's hereabouts at different times were an Italian café and a pub called the Goat in Boots. Writers who knew him well invariably recall meetings in pubs.

As the Chelsea Arts Club was the centre of his literary world in London, so was the annual Cheltenham Festival of Literature in Gloucestershire. For more than thirty years he met his fans there, read his own poems and those of others and basked in the sun of success.

Shelagh Hancox, widow of Alan Hancox, the antiquarian bookseller who was director of the festival from 1980 to 1990 and a friend of Laurie, described how the writer used to sit in her book-lined drawing-room to discuss festival plans. On one occasion the Friends of the Festival had been asked to choose extracts for Laurie to read at a festival event with some pupils from Cheltenham Ladies' College. 'We invited him to a meeting to approve the pieces. Some he seemed to think little of, others he would suggest himself and say the whole poem from memory if we did not know it.'

In the years 1989–93 the Friends produced posters reproducing poems by four leading poets, including Laurie and Seamus Heaney. The poems illustrated the theme of the four elements; the paper was hand-made, the lettering the work of a local printer, the poems headed by wood engravings commissioned from leading artists. Each sold for £50, and Laurie was the guest of honour at a party held in Alan Hancox's bookshop to launch the project.

Another festival venture was the reading of poetry by Laurie and P.J. Kavanagh – a festival director before Alan Hancox – in local churches, among them the famous Norman village church at Elkstone, high on the Cotswolds above Cheltenham and only a few miles from Slad. At the 1981 festival one event featured Laurie and U.A. (Ursula) Fanthorpe reading their poetry as part of an all-day event billed as the 'Poetry Olympics', a marathon relay of poetry reading. Laurie, Ursula Fanthorpe and the audience were supplied with free food and beer. This was good value, since tickets cost just £2.

The 1986 festival came to an end with 'A Celebration for Laurie Lee' at the Everyman Theatre, marking his seventieth birthday a little late. 'This seems a fitting occasion', the programme announced, 'to celebrate his particular changelessness (not that *he* would agree) in a rapidly changing world . . . Laurie himself would hate this to pay homage to a sort of nostalgia.' No fewer than twenty-one distinguished writers took part or sent in contributions. 'We didn't know till the last minute if Laurie would show up,' said Shelagh Hancox. 'Then, just as it was starting, he crept in at the side of the balcony, but he wouldn't appear on stage.' She could not remember Laurie ever giving a solo talk in public, as opposed to undertaking readings or interviews. She speculated that he was too modest to do so, not caring much for the sound of his own voice, even though she found him 'a warm person, a reassuring person to be with'.

Ursula Fanthorpe first made contact with Laurie by letter. 'I was teaching at Cheltenham Ladies' College in the 1970s and I kept asking him to come and read his poems to the school literary society. But there was always some reason why he couldn't come, bronchitis or something. I was interested in the way schoolchildren reacted when they studied his work for exams, so, much later, for one of my poems I invented a child who'd discovered Laurie Lee at school, and I pretended they'd put the poem through my letterbox.'

This was the origin of the now famous 'Dear Mr Lee' poem included in anthologies and in her book of verse *A Watching Brief,* read at festivals and learned by heart for many a poetry competition. Most poets, said the verse, were 'not exactly a laugh a minute' and Shakespeare was 'a national disaster', but *Cider with Rosie* made up for all the others.

The poem went on:

> And I didn't much like those questions
> about social welfare in the rural community
> and the seasons as perceived by an adolescent,
> I didn't think you'd want your book
> read that way, but bits of it I knew by heart,
> and I wish I had your uncles and your half-sisters
> and lived in Slad . . .

It ended: 'P.S. Dear Laurie, please don't feel guilty for me failing the exam, it wasn't your fault . . . I still love *Cider*, it hasn't made any difference.'[4] The poem was commissioned for the Cheltenham Festival, where Ursula Fanthorpe read it to much acclaim. And she related that 'every time we met afterwards he'd say "Have you paid that child any royalties yet?" He never forgot.'

She has published six books of poems and won many awards for her work. In 1994 she became the first woman to be nominated as Professor of Poetry at Oxford. She describes herself as mainly an observer of people, including very sick hospital patients (she worked for some years as a hospital receptionist), and she shares with Laurie a deep love of the Gloucestershire landscape. They met mainly at literary events, where he was quite a lion. 'I admired the sheer achievement of a boy from a not very advantaged home, his sheer enterprise. He was very kind to me, avuncular and genial, in the way of an older writer helping someone younger in the same field.'

The last time she met Laurie was at the Society of Authors, when she won the Cholmondeley Prize for Poetry in 1995 and Laurie presented the awards. 'He grasped my hands and held on, and of course he asked if I'd paid those royalties yet to the child in "Dear Mr Lee". After the main event I found him looking rather old and blind and lost, and we had a chat about Gloucestershire.'

Laurie also had his poems set to music. Johnny Coppin, a singer and songwriter in the folk tradition, first heard Laurie reading some of his poems with Frank Mansell in Cheltenham in the 1970s. Initially he was intrigued mainly by Frank Mansell's work and started setting that writer's poems to music.

Later on the idea dawned on him to record Laurie reading his poetry in his rich baritone. 'He was rather reluctant at first, and he didn't like the sound of his own voice. I used to drive him to Malvern to make the recordings, and he always wanted to come back a long way round through narrow lanes. I suppose they reminded him of his childhood. We had great fun on those drives.'

Once he had secured the readings on record Johnny Coppin began to set the poems to music and to sing them. The rhythms he found difficult, but the imagery and the power of the verse inspired him. 'I love the way he saw familiar things in a new way. He was naturally creative, and I could identify with his poems.' Eventually the musician put together an album, *Edge of Day*, combining Laurie's readings and his own music with violin and recorder accompaniment by Paul Burgess. The effect is extraordinary: Laurie's voice reading passages and linking sung versions of eight of his poems. The recordings are available on tape and compact disc, and they have sold steadily for more than a decade.

Was Laurie cooperative? 'He could be difficult, but he'd come round. We'd meet at his house or the pub, and Kathy would be in the background with cups of tea. Of course he had a great feel for music himself, violin and guitar, and that helped enormously.' Johnny Coppin identifies with Laurie's love of landscape. He told me: 'I can see the apple orchards and my own home valley in his poetry. But I think he was inspired by all kinds of places, not just the Cotswolds and Spain. There are sea images and birds and the seasons in everything he wrote.'

Laurie and the musician appeared together in public twice: during a folk concert at Cheltenham Town Hall, with Laurie as special guest reading his poems, and again as part of the performance held at the Cheltenham Everyman Theatre in 1986 to mark Laurie's seventieth birthday.

After Laurie's death Johnny Coppin and Paul Burgess produced a show developed from the *Edge of Day* album which included extracts from Laurie's three autobiographical books, read by the actor David Goodland.

With advancing years Laurie's fame showed no sign of slackening. The BBC television version of *Cider with Rosie*, first filmed in 1970, was made into a video. Laurie himself began a series of audio tapes reading his own books. Eventually there were six cassettes, three covering *Cider with Rosie* and three from *As I Walked Out One Midsummer Morning*. No actor on earth could match Laurie's voice in telling his own life story.

In 1982 he was admitted as a Freeman of the City of London 'by redemption' – in other words, presentation by someone who had the right to present others as a reward for services. This counted as a conventional freedom, not an honorary one. Members of the City Livery Companies, the Lord Mayor and Aldermen of the City of London are all Freemen, and historically, until the twentieth century, many City Corporation employees were required to be. There is a widespread belief that Freemen of the City of London have the privilege to herd sheep over London Bridge without paying tolls – and Laurie himself told me he thought he could; an appropriate privilege for a Cotswold man. Sadly, the Corporation of London's research guidebook debunks this myth. Laurie was registered as a Freeman in April 1982, being described as an author living in Chelsea. On the certificate his father was named as Reginald Joseph Lee, accountant.

In 1983 a new side of Laurie emerged in public – Laurie Lee, photographer. He had assembled in an album some of his many pictures taken of Kathy and Jessy over the years and added a text as poetic as anything else he wrote. His family meant everything to him, and he could not photograph them enough or write about them too often; more than anything else, *Two Women* demonstrated the depth of his admiration and devotion for Kathy

These were not just family snapshots. Their composition and quality of light remind one of old masters, and some evoke well-known paintings. *Two Women* is a slim but beautifully produced album subtitled *A Book of Words and Pictures* and dedicated 'To my family'. Kathy was portrayed from early womanhood, wearing bikinis (or nothing) in

Mediterranean landscapes, to maturity as an elegant mother cradling a laughing baby. Then came pictures of Jessy in every possible mood: mischievous toddler; pensive five-year-old in a vest; in ringlets aged about twelve; thoughtful adolescent bending intently over her guitar; handsome young woman in ethnic dress.

There were echoes of a Vermeer mother and child, a Renaissance Madonna, Manet's barmaid, an Impressionist's eye view of a girl seen through misted glass. Particularly praised for their originality were photographs showing Kathy, heavily pregnant, feeding milk to a jack-daw and a portrait of Jessy in shades of bronze and auburn strumming her guitar.

Laurie recalled his first meeting with Kathy at Martigues – 'a stumpy, wriggly, golden-haired little girl of five', part English, part French, part Swedish. He met her again in wartime Chelsea, a 'curved and comely' schoolgirl, and became her approved escort. At seventeen she was whisked away to Florence; Laurie cabled a proposal of marriage and sent the fare for her to return.

He described the ups and downs of Kathy's pregnancy and his anxious state waiting for the birth. Then Jessy entered his life. The book ended with an evocation in words and photographs of Jessy dancing, a swirling tempestuous teenager. It balanced the first picture in the book depicting Kathy sensuously curled up on a sea-wall. He summed up their three-way relationship: 'By crowding my days and stealing my sleep they have also lengthened my life.'

Many of the images were shot around Slad – Jessy climbing a field gate, sliding down a mound on Painswick Beacon, propping up a dry-stone wall. One paragraph in particular linked Jessy with her ancestors: 'Another perfect day. I leave my writing-room in Stroud and am met at the bus-stop by mother and daughter with a picnic basket. We go up to Bulls Cross at the head of the valley and sit on an ancient tump overlooking Painswick . . . Took her today to see Auntie Alice in Sheepscombe. Auntie cuddles her fiercely, then bounces her on her knee . . . "I can't master her," she says. "She has a will. Plump, yes, but her flesh is well bestowed."'[5]

The reader can almost hear Laurie's mother's voice as her sister-in-

law speaks, and the place-names – Bulls Cross, Sheepscombe – conjure up generations of Lights some of whose genes have been handed
down to Jessy. And there is a sense of regret that Annie did not live to
see her granddaughter.

In the same year that *Two Women* appeared Laurie published a
book of *Selected Poems* dedicated to Jessy and including most of his
previous verse output published in *The Sun My Monument*, *The Bloom
of Candles* and *My Many-Coated Man*. The introduction could serve
for nearly all Laurie's writings: 'They were written by someone I once
was and who is so distant to me now that I scarcely recognize him any
more. They speak for a time and a feeling which of course has gone
from me, but for which I still have close affection and kinship.'

He was nearly seventy, and several of the last few poems he chose
can be interpreted as dealing with death. In 'Night Speech' he wrote:
'Night, that renews, re-orders/day's scattered dust . . .'; and the last
poem in the collection, 'Fish and Water', brought together his childhood, his travels and a sense of departure: 'As we, who once drank
each other's breath,/Have emptied the air, and gone.'

Even more poignant were the last lines of 'Cock Pheasant': 'For me,
alike, this flushed October . . ./Fevers me fast but cannot fright,
though/Each dropped leaf shows the winter's skull.' It is possible that
Laurie thought of the reissued poems as his literary farewell, not
intending to undertake any more writing. There is evidence that considerable persuasion was needed, from friends and publishers, before
he agreed to embark on the third part of his autobiography.

As British institutions marked his seventieth birthday with tributes,
one was paid in the town in which he had earned his living as a musician and began writing. The citizens of Almuñécar set up their memorial in 1988 to Señor Lorenzo Lee, who had made their town famous
in *As I Walked Out One Midsummer Morning* and *A Rose for Winter*.
Señor Lorenzo kept in touch and still spent occasional holidays there.

His was now a household name among readers. But still he had not
produced his account of the Spanish Civil War – although locals in
Stroud knew he was busy writing when he shut himself away upstairs
at the Subscription Rooms. *A Moment of War* finally came out in 1991

when he was seventy-seven and was published by Viking. Neither he nor they had any idea what a furore the book would arouse after his death.

Tony Lacey, Laurie's editor, described at Laurie's memorial service how the manuscript reached him in 1990: 'I'd been asking him for years about the next part of his autobiography, and he always fobbed me off. So I'd pretty well given up hope. Then we were having a convivial evening and as we tried to grab a taxi he said: "Well, do you want to publish it or don't you?" And soon after that a brown paper parcel arrived, and it turned out to be *A Moment of War.*' Legend has it that in his excitement Lacey accepted the manuscript unread.

A Moment of War was published to much acclaim in 1991. This, said the reviewers, was the long-awaited third part of the trilogy – the hinted-at coda to *Cider with Rosie* and *As I Walked Out One Midsummer Morning*.

It was serialized in the *Observer*. The flashbacks to a half-remembered war nearly sixty years earlier, in a Spain long before most British holidaymakers had discovered it, aroused a great deal of interest. Laurie's particular contribution to European history was to have written as a Gloucestershire countryman caught up in the terrible conflict that was the Spanish Civil War. His view was a poet's view, quite different from the polemics of other International Brigades fighters who had fought an ideological war. Perhaps more than any others who had been there he captured the intense cold, hunger and helplessness of the non-Spanish volunteers.

Reading the short book again, barely 50,000 words, one is struck by the vignettes of extraordinary characters on the Republican side and the bleak horror of the Spanish winter landscape. Take the poet's first view of Teruel: 'a gleaming city of ice . . . a city of silence, without dimension; it could have been a life-size mural, or an intimately carved ivory for some Cardinal or Pope. A perfect relic, in its brilliant stillness, chaste and bloodless as a martyr's tomb. Yet already . . . its citizens were walling up and massacring each other.'

As Edward Blishen wrote in the *Guardian*, it 'aches with unforgotten cold and trembles with unforgotten terror'. Blishen was later to interview Laurie at the Cheltenham Festival about his Spanish memories, but neither then nor in newspaper interviews did Laurie wish to add much to what was written in the book.

For many readers, some of the impact of the book came from the evocative jacket illustration, by Roger Coleman, showing a ragged recruit, rifle on shoulder, gazing across snowfields towards a burning city, and the haunting image of the boy Laurie taken from his rubber-stamped identity card. They reinforced an eloquent story of war.

16

'As Cotswold as a Drystone Wall'

We are, as eyelids fall
And night's silk rises,
stalled in our sleep
to watch the written dark,
brighter than day,
rephrase our stuttered past.

– 'Night Speech'

THE controversy over *A Moment of War* arose only after Laurie's death. His last years were relatively tranquil, with the writer establishing himself as a kind of literary landmark, sought out by tourists and in demand for festivals and arts gatherings all over the south of England. He gave poetry readings and interviews, appeared on radio and television and supported local campaigns to preserve the beauty and quiet of the Cotswolds.

Vernon Scannell knew Laurie well. He recalled a shared television appearance with him in the 1960s, when Laurie arrived at Harlech TV's Bristol studios wearing a baggy tweed suit which the producer felt did not look 'poetic' enough. He intimated as much and Laurie replied: 'I've looked like a yard and a half of old knitting for many years now, and I've no intention of changing.' This was no longer true when he had become a literary elder statesman. Despite his failing eyesight he was very conscious of his appearance in old age and wore dapper suits with stylish scarves and ties. Most typically he sported a Gatsby-style cream suit and elegant panama hat.

He recorded complete readings of *Cider with Rosie* and *As I Walked Out One Midsummer Morning*, packaged as twelve cassettes lasting for over fifteen hours: a formidable task for an eighty-year-old. These were sold in a limited edition of 2,000 copies, each signed personally by the author.

Giving interviews became almost a way of life. Some were given in his Chelsea flat, some in a Chelsea pub, but most were in the Woolpack. Dates and times were fixed, then Laurie would settle in his usual place in the Cider With Rosie Bar – glass at elbow, bag on the floor beside him.

The landlord, David Tarratt, would keep an eye on the progress of the interview, to intervene if it seemed to be going on too long or if drinks were running out. The Woolpack by now was a museum of Lee memorabilia and also a registered bookshop – rumour had it that more copies of *Cider with Rosie* were sold here than anywhere else in Britain. It was well known that on warm days, when he sat on the pub terrace, Laurie would give three rings on his mobile telephone to call for another drink. The landlord knew better than to answer, so the call cost nothing.

Laurie told one interviewer: 'Oh dear, do you really want a photograph of me? I don't look at all like a writer. Nowadays you are meant to wear the uniform of poverty chic, aren't you, a dirty vest and a Porsche?' At the same time he disclosed something of his attitude to women: 'Never declare your love to anyone. Keep them guessing'; and 'At a certain time, as you grow older, you think of Suzie, Anna, Emma, Lucy, Consuela and Maria, and the names radiate pictures that dance round the room. And if you're not able to resurrect these memories with pleasure and gratitude, then you're dead.'[1]

A woman journalist interviewed him at home during the 1980s. He told her that the place was full of locked rooms containing rejected manuscripts and she found 'a heap of letters, lists, bills and poems in a room of unspeakable chaos'. She repeated tales that she had heard of his partiality for spirits, how he fell off the podium at a poetry-reading and smuggled alcohol into these sessions. She repeated yet another variant of the story about the schoolgirls who asked the way to Laurie's grave. (In some versions he told them that he was already in the churchyard, at other times that he was buried in the bar or that he was falling down like an old drystone wall.) He also said he could not write with women around him. 'I often live alone because unlike certain more august writers, like Blake and Dickens, I can't work with women in the room. This is the reason I don't live at home all the time with my dear wife. I love visiting her, then returning to my London fortress where I work.'[2]

He informed the journalist that he had never intended to be a writer. 'I don't even think of myself as a writer now. More a communicator and interpreter of this world and this life . . . which has been a perpetual excitement and joy. No one wants to hear an old poet rambling on about his next book.'

A newspaperman seeking enlightenment found him at Slad 'resplendent in cream jacket, Garrick Club tie and Papa Doc sunglasses'. When he asked Laurie whether certain incidents in *Cider with Rosie* were true he was told: 'It's in the book, isn't it?' He persuaded the newspaperman that he used his white stick 'only to clear a path to the bar' and had his hearing aid tuned to satellite television.

Laurie had once declared that a villager who left his village left it for good, unless he made a fortune and returned as a 'false squire'. The newspaperman asked him: 'Are you a false squire?' and Laurie mischievously replied: 'Well, when I came back I was careful not to buy anyone a drink for two years.'[3]

In an article written in 1994, soon after his eightieth birthday, Laurie wrote: 'I was an imaginative lad, but I could never have foreseen such a turn-up for the books. Pupils who are studying *Cider with Rosie* often arrive with their teachers to be driven round the village in minibuses . . . the churchyard is just across the road from the pub. My mother is buried there and a sister who died at four, and I expect to be buried there myself. It's my valley and I want to be returned to the soil and the roots from which I was born.'[4]

His eightieth birthday was celebrated in many ways. Most memorably there was a television documentary, narrated by Laurie, following a trail around Slad and picking out the landmarks of his boyhood. He revisited what had been the infants' schoolroom, now a comfortably furnished modern sitting-room, recalling where he had sat, which window he had looked out of, how the local lads skated or rabbited or 'whooped through the village like cowboys' after school. By now he had been asked about the 1920s so often that the answers came pat, but they never sounded dull. He was also filmed visiting the grave at Miserden of his old friend Frank Mansell and recalling times with the Three Blind Mice dance band. The film ended with Laurie reciting his own choice of two poems, 'Apples' from *My Many-Coated Man* and 'Field of Autumn' from *The Bloom of Candles*. No one could have read them better.

An interview given to BBC Radio Gloucestershire revealed a little-known aspect of Laurie's character. The interviewer, Mark Hurrell, spent several hours with his tape recorder at Little Court and found Laurie surprisingly nervous for a man so used to being interviewed by print journalists: 'Some parts we had to do several times.' Laurie talked of the vitality of village life. 'It was a life of extreme poverty for most of us, deprivation and disease, but we were like the birds . . . we were a communal ship sailing together, through storms and calms, and we survived.'[5]

Even as children they had been aware of class distinctions. 'The Squire ran the village. Then there were farmers, smallholders, servants, retired butlers, mill workers and farm labourers. But we all belonged, as long as we knew which layer we were in.' The village school was a rewarding start, he reckoned, designed to teach the three R's so that school leavers at least could work in a factory or read a swine disease notice.

He talked also about how he came to literature. The Slad schoolmistress who had called his essay 'high flown' introduced him to poems and folk songs. But his most startling discovery was Stroud Public Library: 'They had Yeats and D.H. Lawrence, and I was going to say Proust, but I don't think we've got Proust there even now. And James Joyce and Huxley opened my eyes to modern literature.' As for his own writing, he believed that a writer could only work on a subject at some distance from it. *Cider with Rosie* had been written in a London attic and *A Moment of War* in Stroud Subscription Rooms, both long after the events described.

The interviewer asked Laurie if he had been naughty or cheeky as a boy. 'You've no right to say that – I was a well-behaved boy' came the answer, just a little too quickly. And had he a great memory for detail? 'I've got a very vivid visual memory, and I can remember sounds. I lost my sense of taste ten or fifteen years ago, but if I'm in a deli and I see a fine home-cured ham all the aromas and flavours are re-created in my dormant senses.'

In another interview soon after his eightieth birthday he admitted to some irritation with people who came to Slad to stare at him: 'Parties come up from Stroud to look round – I try not to get involved. Schoolchildren come because *Cider with Rosie* is a set book. Being a set book is a way of making enemies for life, but I'm charmed if they remember bits of the book and repeat the jokes.' And his love of the Slad Valley was undiminished: 'The same migrating birds come back year after year to the very same bushes. They wouldn't keep coming if they didn't feel this was home, would they? You can still find bee orchids and the chalk blue butterfly. And the blackbirds have a Gloucestershire accent.'[6]

Slad marked Laurie's birthday with a great party – a marquee on the lawn at one of the larger houses, a cake decorated with a violin and a book, champagne and flowers.

Another high point of the 1990s was the wedding of Jessy in May 1990 to a Cheltenham businessman, Damian James. Laurie was very much the proud father, giving her away at Stroud Register Office exactly forty years after his own wedding. As time went on and he travelled less often to London – although he still kept his flat there – he valued a network of old friends mostly living within a ten-mile radius of Slad. Among them were the poets P. J. Kavanagh and Michael Horovitz, the sculptor Lynn Chadwick, the musician Bobby Kok and Laurie's godson Prosper Devas, son of his old friends Anthony and Nicolette Devas.

He was always in demand at local parties and rarely refused an invitation – although Kathy was very protective on these occasions. Invariably Laurie wore his white suit. When he was introduced to a newcomer his opening gambit would almost always be: 'D'ye like living here? Which is your favourite pub?'

He never learned to drive and hated cars. In 1994 he said: 'The village road is a race-track for Ford Sierras, and every cottage has one or two bloated blowfly motor cars encroaching on their gardens.' He looked back to a time when children could play in the road with impunity – if they heard a horse and cart coming they expected the driver to avoid them – and saw the coming of the car as the end of innocence. He accepted a lift or two in old age, but his preferred means of travel was by train.

The Cheltenham Festival of Literature was still an event to which he was always welcomed. He would attend even when he was not on the programme. Another annual fixture was the Congress of the West Country Writers' Association, held each year at various towns around the south-west of England. He was a vice-president of the association. According to its secretary, 'He was a member for as long as anyone could remember because he loved the West Country, and he very rarely missed our annual lunch because he enjoyed the company of other writers. Many of our members have their memories or their favourite stories about him, but he would never give a lecture or an official talk at our Congresses. He spoke often but always off the cuff – a few words at the end of a lunch or a spontaneous response to someone else's speech.'

This was very much the pattern of Laurie's later years. He was an enthusiastic attender of literary events, happy to read his work but reluctant otherwise to speak. On his last appearance at the Cheltenham Festival, in 1995, he was interviewed by Edward Blishen about *A Moment of War* – possibly the nearest he ever came to giving a public lecture. Those who were there will never forget the dramatic unscheduled finale. Laurie walked up to the front of the stage peering out at an unseen audience and waved his white stick. 'I want to thank all you good people for turning out on this mellow autumn evening,' he said. 'Goodbye and God bless you.' It was Laurie's farewell to his fans.

He supported plenty of local campaigns – against traffic and housing developments, against the privatization of the water companies, for conservation and rural life. One of the best remembered in the Stroud area was the battle to save a row of ancient trees threatened by a new supermarket. He invented a jingle, owing a little to his beloved Wordsworth: 'I think that I shall never see a Tesco lovely as a tree.' Opening another, uncontroversial, supermarket he suggested that it would be a good idea if such places had a beer room where husbands could sit while their wives shopped.

In his eighties Laurie's life consisted of social gatherings, local campaigning and an occasional poetry reading or interview. He never refused to sign a copy of one of his books and gave away more than he could count. The signatures invariably carried a personal message.

During 1996 he appeared in public very little, except for an occasional foray to Cheltenham or Cirencester bookshops or a session at the Woolpack. Physically, his health was declining, even if he had not lost his ability to assert himself when he felt it necessary – he forcefully expressed his views on proposals for a housing development in the Painswick Valley; they were later dropped.

Early in 1997 he was admitted to hospital in Gloucester for a major stomach operation, and his friends knew that he was unlikely to make a full recovery. He insisted on being nursed at home, with Kathy and Jessy close by. The end of a rich and fulfilled life came peacefully on 13 May. He died in Slad, not far from his birthplace eighty-three years before. And they buried him, as he had requested, in the village churchyard between the church and the Woolpack. 'Here I am,' he had said in his birthday television programme, 'and here I rest.'

Although the funeral was announced as private, some two hundred people crowded into Holy Trinity Church. As well as family, friends and neighbours, there were familiar faces from Laurie's early years – some schoolfellows, his godson Prosper Devas, his former publisher André Deutsch, friends from his London clubs, the Kavanaghs, representatives of Sheepscombe Cricket Club. Kathy and Jessy led the mourners, and Jack flew over from Australia – the last survivor of Reg's and Annie's talented and remarkable family. Laurie surely would have been glad to know that both his daughters, Jessy and Yasmin, were there to say goodbye, to hear him described by the Vicar of Slad as 'one of us'.

As well as the BBC recording of the memorial service at St James's Church, Piccadilly, there were tribute programmes on radio and television. Two eminent poets provided their own personal tributes to Laurie and read them at the service. Christopher Fry's 'For Laurie Lee' placed him in context as an old friend:

> But how the hell is one to celebrate
> A lifelong, life-imbibing celebrant? . . .
> Treading the grapes of time and people
> He made that earth-engaging tipple
> His vintage Slad.[7]

And Roger McGough had already created what has since become an unforgettable and much quoted epitaph:

> I love the way he uses words;
> Will they work as well for me?
> Sorry, said the words,
> We only do it for Laurie Lee.
> But words are common property,
> They're available and free?
> Sorry, said the words
> We're very choosy
> And we've chosen Laurie Lee.[8]

Stroud honoured its famous son in a music-and-drama presentation at the Victorian Subscription Rooms where he had written most of *A Moment of War*. Local admirers, among them clergy, the MP for Stroud and the town's Mayor, queued to get in. They called it *Windfalls*, and the celebration of Laurie centred on the theme of apples and cider. Street poets, folk musicians, singers and local schools put together a medley of extracts from Laurie's prose and poems set to music. The event would have delighted Laurie. Much free cider was drunk in the interval and a copy of Roger McGough's poem, handwritten by him, was offered as a prize.

At the end of the show Kathy and Jessy stood up to thank the performers and the evening ended with the strains of 'As I Walked Out' played by a single violinist slowly walking from the hall.

Early in 1998 BBC Radio 4 broadcast a newly dramatized version of *Cider with Rosie*, involving schoolchildren from Rodborough and Slad. The actress Niamh Cusack's native Irish accent was transformed into fairly broad Gloucestershire for the part of Annie, while Tim McInnerny, who played Laurie, strangely had no regional accent, despite having been educated at the Marling School – Jack Lee's school. Place and period were evoked by solo folk musicians.

Meanwhile filming was under way in Stroud and several Cotswold villages for a multi-million-pound Carlton Television version of *Cider with Rosie*, with the actress Juliet Stevenson playing Annie. The programme was broadcast in the UK over Christmas 1998. Slad with its garages and conservatories was deemed too modern for exterior location filming, so the village of Sapperton, near Cirencester, stood in for it. Residents awoke to find that their main street had become a gravel track, a camera tower had appeared opposite the Victorian school and a cottage by the school had acquired an inn sign, a brewery board and other paraphernalia to suggest the Woolpack. The scenes inside the inn were partially filmed in Jessy's house, just down the road, as the pub's interior layout had changed since the 1920s. Apparently Laurie's old cottage in Slad could not be used for filming the exterior shots because the owner would not permit it.

Almost exactly a year after his death the West Country Writers' Association, to which Laurie had belonged for more than thirty years, drank a toast to him at their annual meeting. Some members spoke of his loyalty and affection for their organization. Others recalled Laurie the joker: 'He and I used to be drinking rivals on these occasions,' observed a senior literary agent. A veteran historian said: 'He was always heckling the speakers', and a well-known writer of thrillers reminisced: 'Round about now at every meeting Laurie would get up and say: "Well, who's coming to the pub?"'

The association's secretary recalled that one year when Laurie could not attend the annual meeting he telephoned a message which at first they thought had been misspelt as 'Best wishes to you all and especially the immoral Christopher' – a reference to his old friend Christopher Fry, president of the association.

A dozen views of the Slad Valley have been painted by Jack Russell, the England and Gloucestershire cricketer who is also a professional artist. His roots in the valley go as deep as Laurie's. He was born in 1963 in Uplands, a cricket ball's throw from Laurie's birth-place, and his grandmother Nellie Hogg went to Slad village school at around the same time as Laurie. Two of Jack Russell's great-uncles, killed in the First World War, are commemorated on the Slad war memorial: Edward Hogg was drowned at Gallipoli and Harry Hogg died in the trenches. The cricketer's affection for the village led him to buy a cottage close to the Woolpack.

In a 1998 television profile he explained how he felt about land-scape painting: 'I like the English landscape and I'm trying to re-create its atmosphere, whether it's for sunset, dawn light or reflections in water.' *Cider with Rosie* offered him considerable inspiration, and he was filmed painting Slad scenes, among them Jones's pond where Miss Flynn was said to have drowned.

Jack Russell is sad that he never met Laurie. He wrote to arrange a meeting and Laurie had replied: 'Dear boy, come any time' – but some-how the meeting never materialized. Jack painted Laurie's grave from a viewpoint in Holy Trinity churchyard soon after the funeral. 'This is his final resting place, looking across the valley at the Woolpack.'

At the end of the 1990s Laurie's books still sell around the world. In the United States three titles remain in print: *As I Walked Out One Midsummer Morning*, *A Moment of War* and *Selected Poems*. (*Edge of Day* is the American title given to *Cider with Rosie*, alcoholic cider being hardly known in the United States.) In France, translations of *Cider with Rosie* and *As I Walked Out One Midsummer Morning* are still available, and in Spain *Cider with Rosie* and *A Moment of War* are in print: *As I Walked Out One Midsummer Morning* is no longer available. As for the fourteen other languages into which Laurie's books have been translated, it is hard to find any now. Laurie was heard to say: 'When I ask my publishers about rights and royalties and things they usually say, oh, there are one or two still on sale in China.'

In the last few years Laurie's world has begun to change. First to go were the contents of the flat at Elm Park Gardens. An auction was held, and his much-used typewriter fetched £45. Fans of Laurie's writ-ings said they would have given much more for it if they had been there. Next, his home from home, the Woolpack Inn, came on the market. David Tarratt, Laurie's friend and unofficial public relations officer there for many years, decided to retire. 'I really believe that whoever buys it will keep the pub the way it is,' he told me. 'There's a huge tourist business here and it's going to get bigger. People keep coming and asking to see where Laurie sat – or sits, if they don't know he's died.'

Two years after Laurie's funeral wake was held at the Woolpack, the pub still had his books for sale in a glass case; the Cider With Rosie Bar remains home to a variety of folk music groups; the walls are dotted with pictures of Slad past and present, photographs of Laurie and his funeral, as well as displays of his book jackets. It is a one-man folk museum.

The other major change has been the loss of the pub's early nineteenth-century oak settle where Laurie and Frank Mansell used to sit. It graced the Woolpack for perhaps fifty years, and brass plaques with the names of Laurie, Frank and a previous landlord, Richard Covington, had been attached to it. In the late 1980s two antique dealers and a restorer were drinking in the bar. Overhearing their chat, the landlord mentioned that he had an old settle in the barn; it had been cleared out to make room for more tables. One of the dealers snapped it up and the settle went to Scotland. Laurie was not pleased when he found out about the sale. The other dealer and the restorer later bought shares in it and in 1997 one of them arranged for it to return to Gloucestershire in the hope that it would find a permanent home in its native county. Thus it found its way into the window of a bookshop in Dursley where it was advertised for sale for £2,000. The bookshop closed in 1998, and the settle found a temporary home in Stratford-upon-Avon. To date, it is still up for sale.

In spite of changes, other aspects of Laurie's world retain their character. Slad village has farms, cottages and fields that Laurie knew as a child. Externally the Woolpack has changed very little. Out of the pub window you can look across the valley to a farm landscape in one direction and in the other across to the churchyard where one of the most recent graves is his, smothered in flowers.

Innumerable tributes were paid to Laurie after his death. An anonymous Australian visitor wrote on a card at Slad church: 'Thank you, Laurie, for *Cider with Rosie*.' His Stroud friend and bookseller, Alan Tucker, wrote a poem, 'Laurie Lee in Stroud', which ends:

> Returning home through the summer once a week or so
> an ancient revered figure appears at the station entrance.
> He peers to left and right looking for his wife.
> If, as usual, he fails to find her, slowly
> he makes his way to the Imperial Hotel bar
> where he orders a malt. When Kathy arrives, eventually,
> late, he stands Buddha-like at the pavement's edge
> at once seraphic and carefully looking nowhere,
> a man facing a firing squad made up entirely of friends.

17

Laurie Remembered

Death's family likeness in each face
must show, at last, our brotherhood.

        – 'The Long War'

RIENDS' memories of Laurie are as diverse as the people themselves. From their recollections can be assembled a composite picture of a complex man, much loved but meaning different things to
different people.

Jacqueline Thomson (now Lady Tucker), widow of Laurie's close
friend and illustrator, the Canadian artist Bill Thomson, was impressed
by his kindness. 'When my daughter Hannah was born in 1975 Laurie
gave her a Krugerrand as a christening present. These were gold coins
– people were collecting them – and I was told it was worth about
£200. I don't know how Laurie acquired it – maybe someone brought
it back from South Africa. It was very generous of him.'

Her husband had come to Britain as an art student in 1947, and he
met Laurie soon after, probably at Finch's pub in the Fulham Road
where many of the Queen's Elm set used to gather before Sean Treacy
moved to the Queen's Elm. In the 1950s Laurie and Kathy, Bill Thomson and his first wife Margaret went on holiday to Spain together. Margaret was the daughter of the writer Henry Williamson, and she later
married the guitarist and lutenist Julian Bream, who played memorably in the film version of *As I Walked Out One Midsummer Morning*.

Lady Tucker especially remembered Laurie's practical jokes and
mischievous sense of humour. She tells of the dinner party she gave for
a friend, where Laurie stood up and recited a story of a blind flute
player. The accompanying actions involved some manual dexterity
with his flies, which brought the house down. In spite of his sense of

fun, however, Laurie could be moody, she observed, and he would sometimes hide behind a partition at the pub to avoid meeting people. 'He was a born tease to the end of his life,' she said. When his sight was failing a neighbour used to escort him to the Chelsea Arts Club and acted as his minder: 'But he pretended his sight and hearing were worse than they were; he could spot a good shot at snooker quite easily.'

Adam Horovitz, son of poets Michael and the late Frances Horovitz, offers a young writer's perspective on Laurie. Adam was born in 1971, when Laurie was fifty-seven, and came to live in the next hamlet to Slad as a baby. Michael was an old friend of Laurie's from the Chelsea Arts Club. 'He was a great man, and something of a mentor to me. When I decided I wanted to be a poet my father said: "Good grief, Adam, get yourself a proper job", but Laurie said: "Don't take any notice. You do your own thing." When he came to our house he'd stuff fifty pence pieces in my hand and say: "Have you written any poems recently?" And everyone's heard the story about my meeting him outside Stroud Station when he gave me a fiver and said: "Go and get drunk, my boy, and write some poems."'

Adam Horovitz is a member of the Stroud group of young poets who do performance poetry at festivals. 'Laurie was good at communicating with young people. He didn't talk down to us, and he often supported our events.' He has a high regard for Laurie's poems, which he rates more highly than his prose, and he suggests the reason for their being relatively overlooked is that nature poetry is 'somewhat snobbishly' discredited at the present time. 'His poetry is beautiful. I loved hearing him read it. In the sixties my father and he used to read their poems to jazz – I'd have liked to have heard that.'

Alan and Joan Tucker, Stroud booksellers, knew Laurie for more than thirty years. Joan Tucker told me how she met him. 'It was in September 1962. There was a country house sale near Stonehouse, and I was looking for second-hand books. We chatted afterwards at the bus stop – I recognized Laurie, and I told him we were just opening a new bookshop. On our very first day there was a present on the doorstep: a signed copy of *The Bloom of Candles*, and the message

"Good Luck". Later on he brought us another six copies, a special edition, numbered and corrected by hand.'

Her husband added that Laurie called often at the shop, always teasingly carrying the bag of a rival bookshop. 'When it was falling to bits we said that he had better go back to Cheltenham and buy another book there. He is by far our best-selling author, and all his books still sell.' Even in his old age Laurie undertook signings for the Tuckers and also for Woolworth's and W.H. Smith, the two local bookshops mentioned in his early essay 'True Adventures of the Boy Reader'.

Regular early callers at the Tuckers' second-hand bookshop were Laurie and Frank Mansell. Alan Tucker recalled: 'They were inseparable buddies. I arranged readings for them both at the Subscription Rooms, but it was very rare for Laurie to give a talk. Once the Western Bookmen, a group of publishers' representatives, held their annual meeting in this area, and Laurie was invited to give a humorous talk; but he wouldn't. Another time the manager of a local hotel arranged a Laurie Lee Weekend, with walks and talks. Laurie agreed to sign books as long as he got a good dinner.' To Alan Tucker he was unique – 'a canny countryman. He could weave stories you always took with a pinch of salt. Whatever he said, there was a twinkle in his eye.'

Bernard Stone, a Kensington and Covent Garden bookseller, remembered Laurie as 'a delightful fellow with a little mischievous streak'. He sold many of Laurie's books, arranged popular signings and published several Lee poems as broadsheets. They met around 1970 at the Chelsea Arts Club and became good friends in the fraternity that gravitated around the Arts Club and the Queen's Elm. The bookseller offered a rare glimpse of Laurie at work. 'We arranged to meet at a Fulham Road pub, I think the Rose, and there he was writing away with a Ruddles and a whisky chaser at his elbow. The pub jukebox was blaring out, but he didn't seem at all bothered by it.'

Most of Laurie's friends recalled his fondness for alcohol. His books and articles seldom fail to mention the *vin du pays*: in Slad it was cider, in Spain it was cognac and rough red wine, in Cyprus the local wine, in London 'a tot of whisky'. At home he must have missed the relaxed street café life and cheap drinks of Mediterranean countries. Even in Beirut he was charmed by the ambience of the Mayflower Hotel: 'Built into the hotel there is also the Duke of Wellington, the proprietor's dream of an English pub.' In Jamaica he had free rum punch; at an Irish medieval-style banquet there were 'flagons of claret to follow up the mead'.

In England pubs were his clubs: the Rose in Kensington (where he took his own tankard in his briefcase), hostelries up and down the King's Road in Chelsea and of course the Cotswold pubs with occupational names – the Carpenters' Arms, the Butchers' Arms, the Fleece, the Ram, the Shunters. In pubs he talked to anyone and everyone or invited friends to join him. For him the pub or alehouse was always the centre of life. In 1988 he said: 'One never says one's deaf, you know, as one never says one's an alcoholic. Incidentally, my GP recently asked me what I'd drunk that day and I replied: "Two beers and a short", which is alcoholic code for fifteen beers and half a bottle of whisky.'

To his enormous circle of friends Laurie was a social drinker, a person they would happily listen to for hours over a glass or two, reminiscing over the past, deploring some aspects of the present, but always with the wit and articulacy of a poet. He drew together his two pleasures in an epigram: 'I tend to think of white wine as the sharp blonde, and red as the dark comforting brunette.'

Very few people ever saw Laurie writing. He shut himself away, keeping regular writing hours, often an eight-hour day, and never discussed his books with anyone. Occasionally a poem would emerge as a gift.

He was a painstaking writer, crafting a page over and over again until he was happy with it. The first edition of *Cider with Rosie*, running to 280 pages, took him nearly four years, and there was a twenty-year gap before *As I Walked Out One Midsummer Morning* appeared. Opinion is divided as to whether he mostly wrote by hand or mostly typed, but it is likely that he typed first, then revised by hand. Kathy has spoken of finding a forgotten manuscript with one paragraph written out twenty times on separate bits of paper.

His writing was solitary, created with effort, meticulous. Nicolette

Devas said he did not seek out facts because he feared they might keep his imagination earthbound: not a criticism that many readers would level at Laurie.

Barbara Tait, chairwoman of Painswick Parish Council, is a distant relative of Laurie through his Light ancestors. She was born in Sheepscombe and remembers his mother Annie calling at her home, Clissold Farm, in the late 1940s. 'I remember her as happy-go-lucky and talkative.' In recent years she used to meet Laurie when he came to the chairman's reception at Painswick Town Hall. 'He came every year; a wonderful character, very amusing – and rather a ladies' man.'

Residents of Painswick say that some years ago Laurie was the generous giver of sixpences to all the local children who took part in the village's annual churchyard yew-clipping festival, and he was certainly generous with his time as prize-giver at the Painswick Horticultural Show.

Kathy looked back on forty-seven years of marriage as a wife who had unfailingly been Laurie's stay and support, but she was modest about her role: 'I might have made life a little more comfortable for him, but he would have written somehow or other.'[1] The move to Rose Cottage in Slad in 1962 changed her life dramatically. From being a cosmopolitan Londoner she had to adapt to the slower rhythms and close-knit community life of Gloucestershire. She settled in happily, driving Laurie everywhere he needed to go, becoming a churchwarden and supporter of that bastion of rural life, the Women's Institute. And she adapted to motherhood, too.

Some eight years after arriving in Slad, when Jessy was six, the Lees bought Little Court, an old house tucked into the side of the valley just below the Woolpack, and they never moved again. Jessy transferred from a private school in London to Cheltenham Ladies' College. Weekends were always spent by the family at Little Court, even when Laurie stayed in London writing during the week.

Kathy describes her husband as having been a romantic, a good listener and a secret giver to good causes, devoted to her and Jessy. He always valued their opinions. 'He was a very fatherly creature really, as I was so much younger than him.'

A picture emerges of a complex and contradictory man, sometimes secretive and moody, at others incredibly generous as well as witty and amusing. He was wise and articulate, yet many of his friends say he seldom initiated a conversation and was difficult to get to know well. 'You had to make all the going,' said Alan Ross. Laurie professed to dislike London, yet he spent at least half of each week and most of his social life there. His books sold by the million, yet he often called anxiously at bookshops to ask how they were doing. He had a habit of turning up late, or not at all, when he was expected to be the star turn. And almost everyone remembered his practical jokes and gentle teasing, his armour against the world.

Some say he preferred to drink with other men, yet no one denies that all his life he sparkled and glowed in women's company. He was convivial, gregarious but always a little wary. Comments by people in the Stroud area who knew him varied from 'cantankerous' to 'an absolute charmer'.

His approach to life was encompassed in his poems, and it is there we should search for the beliefs that inspired him, his inner voice and interior landscape. In 'The Wild Trees' he wrote of the dialect of the hills and his wish 'to sleep with the coiled fern leaves in the heart's live stone'.

Although he wrote so much about himself there were areas of his life he kept wholly private, and Laurie-in-London was a different man from Laurie-in-Slad; but always he was kind and considerate, never refusing help when it was asked of him. Those who met him for the first time were captivated. Wherever he found himself, Laurie's greatest pleasure was to be welcomed into the company as a friend. The way he wished the world to see him can be summed up in the words he exchanged with the Republican soldier who challenged him on the border of wartime Spain: 'I've come to join you.' '*Pase usted.*'

Notes

Chapter 1

1. Vita Sackville-West in *An Illustrated Survey of Berkeley Castle*, English Life Publications, Derby, 1990, p. 2.
2. *Kelly's Directory of Gloucestershire and Bristol*, Kelly's Directories, Bristol, 1892, pp. 669, 880, 897–900.
3. Documents held at Dorset County Archives Service, Dorchester.
4. Laurie Lee, 'Writing Autobiography', *New York Times Book Review*, 30 August 1964, reprinted in *I Can't Stay Long*, André Deutsch, London, 1975.

Chapter 2

1. C.H. Warren, *A Cotswold Year*, Geoffrey Bles, London, 1936, reprinted by Alan Sutton, Gloucester, 1985, pp. 14–15, 18.
2. Warren, p. 62.
3. Ivor Gurney, *Collected Letters*, Carcanet Press, Manchester, 1991, pp. 153, 484, 513.

Chapter 3

1. *Gloucestershire Echo*, 14 November 1994.
2. *Daily Telegraph*, 27 July 1994.

Chapter 4

1. References to Slad history taken from *The Story of Our Village 1850–1957*, Slad Women's Institute, Slad, 1957.
2. Head Teacher's Log Book, Slad Village School, 1917–25; manuscript held in Gloucester County Record Office, Gloucester.
3. Letter in possession of the family.
4. Interview with the author, 14 November 1994.
5. Laurie Lee, 'True Adventures of the Boy Reader', in the *New York Times Book Review*, 12 November 1961, reprinted in *I Can't Stay Long*.

Chapter 5

1. W.O. Wicks, *Marling School 1887–1987*, Oxford University Press, Oxford, 1986, pp. 238–40, 245.
2. *Laurie Lee's Gloucestershire*, Channel 4 television programme, transmitted 1994.
3. Letter to the author, 27 October 1997.
4. Interview on BBC Radio Gloucestershire, 30 May 1994.
5. Frank Mansell, *Cotswold Ballads*, introduction by Laurie Lee, privately published 1969; reprinted by R. Courtauld, Stroud, 1974.
6. Laurie Lee, 'First Love', in *Vogue*, c. 1960, reprinted in *I Can't Stay Long*.

Chapter 7

1. David and Anna Kenning, *En Los Pasos de Laurie Lee*, Casa de Galicia, Madrid, 1996.
2. Roy Campbell, *Light on a Dark Horse*, Hollis and Carter, London, 1969.
3. *Today*, 3 January 1987.
4. Maria Carlota Palm, 'Almuñécar en la obra de Laurie Lee en el recuerdo de sus habitantes', *Al-Munecab*, Antigua Sexi IES [Institute of Educational Studies of Old Almuñécar], Almuñécar, 1997, pp. 7–9.
5. *Today*, 3 January 1987.

Chapter 8

1. Jack Jones, *Union Man*, Collins, London, 1986, pp. 64, 66, 75–6.
2. Letter to the author, 1 March 1998.
3. Walter Gregory, *The Shallow Grave*, Gollancz, London, 1986, pp. 25–6, 58, 97–8.
4. George Orwell, *Homage to Catalonia*, Secker and Warburg, London, 1938, p. 25.
5. Hugh Thomas, *The Spanish Civil War*, Eyre and Spottiswoode, London, 1961, p. 711.
6. *The Times*, 1 January 1998.
7. Simon Courtauld, *Spectator*, 3 January 1998.
8. Barry McLoughlin, *Guardian*, 3 January 1998.
9. Barry McLoughlin, letter to the author, 9 January 1998.

Chapter 9

1. Jack Lee, letter to the author, 25 December 1997.
2. John Mortimer, *Clinging to the Wreckage*, Weidenfeld and Nicolson, London, 1982, pp. 92–5.
3. Sean Day-Lewis, *C. Day-Lewis: A Literary Life*, Weidenfeld and Nicolson, London, 1980, pp. 148–9, 154, 171, 199.
4. Rosamond Lehmann, *Rosamond Lehmann's Album*, Chatto and Windus, London, 1985, p. 72.
5. *Horizon*, April, May, July 1940; December 1943; December 1945; April 1946.
6. Alan Ross, *Coastwise Lights*, Collins Harvill, London, 1988, p. 219.
7. Nicolette Devas, *Two Flamboyant Fathers*, Collins, London, 1966, pp. 249–54.
8. *Daily Telegraph*, 27 July 1994.

Chapter 11

1. Christopher Fry, letter to the author, 21 July 1997.
2. *Daily Telegraph*, 15 May 1997.
3. Laurie Lee, 'An Obstinate Exile', BBC Third Programme radio talk, c. 1950, reprinted in *I Can't Stay Long*.

Chapter 12

1. Stephen Gardiner, *Epstein*, Flamingo, London, 1993, pp. xi, 340, 415.
2. Interview with the author, 1998.
3. M. Hanham and B. Hillier (eds), *A Tonic for the Nation*, Thames and Hudson, London, 1976, pp. 165, 181, 187.
4. Christopher Barry, letter to the author, 30 August 1998.
5. P.J. Kavanagh, letter to the author, 25 July 1997.
6. *A Tribute to Laurie Lee*, BBC Radio Gloucestershire, 20 May 1994.

Chapter 13

1. Laurie Lee, 'Ibiza High Fifties', *Encounter* magazine, c. 1955, reprinted in *I Can't Stay Long*.
2. Lee, 'Writing Autobiography'.
3. Martyn Harris, *Daily Telegraph*, 27 July 1994

4. Lee, 'Writing Autobiography'.

5. *Stroud News*, 13 November 1959.

6. *Daily Telegraph*, 18 November 1959.

7. Jim Fern, *Ferns in the Valley*, Millvale, Evesham, 1994, pp. 13, 22.

8. *Gloucestershire Echo*, 14 November 1994.

9. *Evening Standard*, 28 October 1960.

Chapter 14

1. Laurie Lee, *Two Women*, André Deutsch, London, 1983, pp. 36–7.

2. Laurie Lee, 'The Firstborn', *Evening Standard* (London), 1964, reprinted in *I Can't Stay Long*.

3. Laurie Lee, *The Gypsies of Granada*, Athelnay Books, London, 1969, pp. 9–11.

4. Campbell, *Light on a Dark Horse*, pp. vi–vii.

5. *Spectator*, 8 August 1998.

Chapter 15

1. *Laurie Lee's Gloucestershire* (Channel 4).

2. *Daily Telegraph Magazine*, 20 February 1976.

3. Tom Cross, *Artists and Bohemians*, Quiller Press, London, 1992.

4. U.A. Fanthorpe, *A Watching Brief*, Peterloo Poets, Cornwall, 1987, pp. 22–3.

5. Lee, *Two Women*, p. 75.

Chapter 16

1. *Guardian*, 1 January 1998.

2. *Today*, 3 January 1987.

3. *Daily Telegraph*, 18 February 1988.

4. *Daily Telegraph*, 27 July 1994.

5. *Daily Mail*, 22 January 1994.

6. *A Tribute to Laurie Lee* (BBC Radio Gloucestershire).

7. Christopher Fry, *Sunday Times*, 25 May 1997 (Book Section).

8. Roger McGough, poem first read on Channel 4 television, May 1994.

Chapter 17

1. Kathy Lee, interviewed in *You* magazine, 20 September 1998.

Chronological List of Writings

The Dead Village (adapted from a poem by Viktor Fischl), London: Young
Czechoslovakia, 1943

The Sun My Monument (poems), London: Hogarth Press, 1944

Land at War (Ministry of Information publication), London: HMSO, 1945

Peasants' Priest (play), Canterbury: H.J. Goulden, 1947

The Bloom of Candles (poems), London: Hogarth Press, 1947

Vassos the Goatherd (adapted from a film by John Maddison), London: Pilot
Press, 1947

We Made a Film in Cyprus, London: Longmans Green, 1947

The Voyage of Magellan: A Dramatic Chronicle for Radio, London: John
Lehmann, 1948

A Rose for Winter, London: Hogarth Press, 1955

My Many-Coated Man (poems), London: Hogarth Press, 1955

Ireland, Geoffrey, A Camera Study of the Artist at Work (Introduction by
Laurie Lee), London: André Deutsch in association with the Royal
Academy of Arts, 1958

Cider with Rosie, London: Hogarth Press, 1959

The Firstborn, London: Hogarth Press, 1964, a part of which appeared
originally in the Evening Standard (London), 1964

As I Walked Out One Midsummer Morning, London: André Deutsch,
1969

The Gypsies of Granada (writings and drawings), London: Athelnay Books,
1969

Roy Campbell, Light on a Dark Horse (Foreword by Laurie Lee), London:
Hollis and Carter, 1969

Frank Mansell, Cotswold Ballads (Introduction by Laurie Lee), privately
published, 1969

Pergamon Poets Ten (with Charles Causley), Oxford: Pergamon Press,
1970

I Can't Stay Long (essays), London: André Deutsch, 1975

Two Women (text with photographs), London: André Deutsch, 1983
Selected Poems, London: André Deutsch, 1983
A Moment of War, London: Viking, 1991

Note: This list does not include single poems or articles published in magazines or newspapers.

Filmography

Spare Time, GPO Film Unit, London, 1939 (script by Laurie Lee)

Close Quarters, Crown Film Unit, 1940 (script partly by Laurie Lee)

Cyprus Is an Island, Ministry of Information, 1946 (script by Laurie Lee)

A Tale in a Tea Cup, Green Park Film Unit, 1947 (script by Laurie Lee)

West of England, Festival of Britain, 1951 (script by Laurie Lee)

Journey Into Spring, British Transport Library, 1957 (script by Laurie Lee)

Cider with Rosie, BBC, 1971

Return to Rosie, HTV, 1979

As I Walked Out One Midsummer Morning, BBC2, 1987 (presented by Laurie Lee)

A Rose for Winter, BBC, 1989

Great Western Writers in Residence, HTV, 1994

Laurie Lee's Gloucestershire, Channel 4, 1994 (narrated by Laurie Lee)

Cider with Rosie, Carlton TV, 1998

Index